Ashtavakra Gita

Word-for-Word Translation from Sanskrit by

Janki Parikh

ISBN: 978-172-86-0479-4

Copyright © 2015 Janki Parikh

All rights reserved. This book or any portion thereof may not be reproduced or used in any manner whatsoever without the express written permission of the publisher except for the use of brief quotations in a book review or scholarly journal.

Publisher contact: info@jankiparikh.com

www.jankiparikh.com

ASHTAVAKRA GITA

Contents

Copyright	Ii
Introduction	1
Text and Translation	3
Chapter One	4
Chapter Two	11
Chapter Three	19
Chapter Four	24
Chapter Five	26
Chapter Six	28
Chapter Seven	30
Chapter Eight	32
Chapter Nine	34
Chapter Ten	37
Chapter Eleven	40
Chapter Twelve	43
Chapter Thirteen	46
Chapter Fourteen	49
Chapter Fifteen	51
Chapter Sixteen	58
Chapter Seventeen	62
Chapter Eighteen	69
Chapter Nineteen	102
Chapter Twenty	105

Introduction

Who are you? Are you your body, your personality, your special talents and achievements?

What do you seek? Is it wealth, love, security, recognition, deeper meaning? Are you convinced that having more and more of all of this is the goal of one's life, that there is lasting happiness somewhere during or at the end of this quest?

What if someone were to tell you that you are none of these things, and that all the things you seek are merely poor, insubstantial reflections of that which is your ultimate goal...

…that YOU are that which you seek, YOU are the only one desperate quest of your life, and YOU are the only one final answer of your life?

This is not some new-born, 2-day-old philosophy. This ancient philosophy is thousands of years old. This is the essence of the Vedas, the Upanishads, the Brahma Sutras; this is the foundation of life itself!

Awaken to Advaita, the principle of non-duality... awaken to your true SELF! Allow Sage Ashtavakra to guide you on an incredible, astonishing journey of self-realization, just as he guides King Janaka in this short dialogue of 20 chapters known as the Ashtavakra Gita.

What's the connection between King Janaka and Sage Ashtavakra? Here's the story….

TRANSLATED BY JANKI PARIKH

The Story of Ashtavakra and Janaka

King Janaka, the great, just and popular, learned, many-talented and sensitive king had a powerful dream one night. He dreamt his kingdom was suddenly under attack by a vicious enemy. The King, along with his generals, fought a valiant battle, but lost badly to the ferocious enemy. Defeated and exhausted, Janaka was taken prisoner and brought before the enemy king, who laughed at him and exiled him from his own kingdom.

Now King Janaka – wounded, hungry, thirsty, exhausted – wandered along the outskirts of his kingdom. People who were his own subjects just a while ago refused to even give him water out of fear of the new king!

Then a beggar took pity on him and offered him the watery remains of a meal. Grateful, King Janaka took his wretched bowl and thanked the beggar. But as soon as he was about to eat it, a bird pounced upon the earthen pot and broke it! This was the last straw. King Janaka gave in to his misery and collapsed in a heap – cursing his fate, crying… an utterly broken man…

And then…

Janaka woke up…

…And found himself on his own bed, safe in his golden palace, surrounded by his loyal guards in his beloved kingdom! Seeing the King so disturbed, the guards summoned the ministers, who gathered in his chamber immediately asking with concern, "What happened Maharaj?"

But Janaka just sat in a trance, completely overpowered by his realistic dream. After a few moments, he muttered, "Was that real or is this real?"

Nobody could understand his question or the depth of the angst behind it. But he wouldn't say anything else. Everyone who approached him out of concern – the ministers, the queen, the well-wishers, the royal doctors, the court scholars – they all got only a desperate plea in return for their efforts, "Was that real or is this real?"

This continued for a few days. He would not say anything else to anyone even in court. His frantic query reverberated everywhere… "Was that real or is this real?"

Rumours now spread thick and fast throughout the kingdom that the king had gone off his rocker. Incidentally, the great sage Ashtavakra was passing by the capital city at that time. He too heard the stories of King Janak's mysterious state. He then decided to go and meet the king himself.

Sage Ashtavakra – born with eight (ashta) severe birth defects causing his body to be unnaturally bent (vakra) – was still the most majestic of all men, as he walked into the court with his bowed legs. His intense spirituality shone like a halo around his face, and the whole court fell silent!

"Was that real or is this real?" asked King Janaka. Ashtavakra understood in a trice what no on had understood so far.

He asked Janaka, "When you were in THAT state – covered in dust, wounded, hungry, thirsty, depressed and miserable, was THIS current state also with you – your queen, your palace, your ministers and well-wishers, your power?

The king's eyes came alive for the first time in days, and he said, "No, this wasn't there then."

Ashtavakra said, "And now during THIS state – surrounded by your queen, your palace, your ministers and comfort, are you still experiencing THAT state – dirt, hunger, thirst, misery?"

"No," said the King.

"Then it's simple O King. If THAT doesn't always exist, and THIS doesn't always exist, then neither this nor that is real!" proclaimed Ashtavakra smiling.

Shocked, Janaka asked, "What? Is nothing real then?"

"Janaka, were YOU present during your experience of misery, hunger, thirst, defeat?" asked Ashtavakra.

"Yes," said Janaka, the light beginning to dawn…

"And are YOU present here now, in this state of power and comfort?
"Yes, I am".

"Then Dear King, neither this is real, nor that is real. Only YOU are real!"

A collective gasp went around the court, as the first flame of self-knowledge lit up in Janaka's heart.

Who is this ME, this experiencer of various states, this witness who always exists no matter what? Who am I? WHO AM I?

This is the starting point of the Ashtavakra Gita. Through each of the chapters, Ashtavakra takes Janaka further and further into the discovery of this "I", this SELF, this eternal witness.

Ashtavakra, the brilliant, self-realized sage with eightfold physical deformities, is simple, straightforward, even harsh throughout this dialogue. He does not mince words, he does not bother with niceties. His only aim is to get the message across to his worthy pupil – which he does, more effectively than any flowery speech ever could! With the aim of a master archer beyond compare, he pierces Janaka's heart and mind. A true-blue guru, indeed!

This ancient book has been a favourite of great sages, seers and gurus throughout the centuries, including Ramakrishna Paramahamsa, Swami Vivekananda, Ramana Maharshi, Sarvapalli Radhakrishnan, Sri Sri Ravi Shankar, to name a few.

King Janaka found his enlightenment at the end of the dialogue. Now reach out and find yours!

Note: This work is meant to be a literal translation of the original Sanskrit text. I believe it is important to preserve the integrity of the original work, which is why I have made every attempt to stay true to the meaning of each verse, to the best of my abilities.

TRANSLATED BY JANKI PARIKH

Text and Translation

Chapter 1

जनक उवाच
कथं ज्ञानमवाप्नोति कथं मुक्तिर्भविष्यति।
वैराग्य च कथं प्राप्तमेतद ब्रूहि मम प्रभो ॥१-१॥

janaka uvacha
katham gyanam avapnoti katham muktirbhavishyati |
vairagya cha katham praptam etad bruhi mama prabho ||1-1||

King Janaka said –
O venerable one, please tell me how does one obtain wisdom? How does one become liberated? How does one achieve detachment?

अष्टावक्र उवाच
मुक्तिमिच्छसि चेतात् विषयान विषवत्त्यज।
क्षमार्जवदयातोष सत्यं पीयूषवद्भज ॥१-२॥

ashtavakra uvacha
muktim ichhasi chettat vishayana vishavattyaja |
kshama arjava dayatosha satyam piyushavad bhaja ||1-2||

Ashtavakra said –
If you wish to be liberated, renounce the objects of the senses as poison. Worship forgiveness, honesty, compassion, contentment and truth as nectar.

न पृथ्वी न जलं नाग्निर्न वायुर्द्यौर्न वा भवान्।
एषां साक्षिणमात्मानं चिद्रूपं विद्धि मुक्तये ॥१-३॥

na pruthvi na jalam nagnirna vayurdyaurna va bhavan |
esham sakshinam atmanam chidrupam viddhi muktaye ||1-3||

You are neither the earth, nor water, nor fire, nor air, nor space. In order to be liberated, know yourself as pure consciousness, the witness of all these.

यदि देहं पृथक् कृत्य चिति विश्राम्य तिष्ठसि।
अधुनैव सुखी शान्तो बन्धमुक्तो भविष्यसि ॥१-४॥

yadi deham pruthak krutya chiti vishramya tishthasi |
adhunaiva sukhi shanto bandhamukto bhavishyasi ||1-4||

If you detach yourself from the body and rest in consciousness, you immediately become happy, peaceful and free from bondage.

न त्वं विप्रादिको वर्ण: नाश्रमी नाक्षगोचर:।
असङ्गोऽसि निराकारो विश्वसाक्षी सुखी भव ॥१-५॥

na tvam vipradiko varnah nashrami naksha gocharah |
asango asi nirakaro vishvasakshi sukhi bhava ||1-5||

You are not a Brahmin or any other caste, you do not belong to any life-stage (four ashramas - Brahmacharya, Grihastha, Vanaprastha, Sannyas), nor are you limited to what can be perceived by the eyes. You are unattached, formless, and the witness of all things. Therefore, be happy.

धर्माधर्मौ सुखं दुखं मानसानि न ते विभो।
न कर्तासि न भोक्तासि मुक्त एवासि सर्वदा ॥१-६॥

dharma adharmau sukham dukham manasani na te vibho |
na kartasi na bhoktasi mukta evasi sarvada ||1-6||

Righteousness, unrighteousness, joy and sorrow belong to the mind, not to your eternal Self. You are neither the doer, nor the enjoyer. You are always undeniably free!

एको द्रष्टासि सर्वस्य मुक्तप्रायोऽसि सर्वदा।
अयमेव हि ते बन्धो द्रष्टारं पश्यसीतरम् ॥१-७॥

eko drashtasi sarvasya muktaprayo asi sarvada |
ayameva hi te bandho drashtaram pashyasitaram ||1-7||

You are the solitary witness of all that is, forever abundantly free. Your only bondage is perceiving the witness as someone other than yourself.

अहं कर्तेत्यहंमान महाकृष्णाहिदंशितः।
नाहं कर्तेति विश्वासामृतं पीत्वा सुखं भव ॥१-८॥

aham kartetyaham mana mahakrushnahidamshitah |
naham karteti vishvasamrutam pitva sukham bhava ||1-8||

The thought "I am the doer" is like the bite of a greatly poisonous snake. Faith that "I am not the doer" is nectar. Drink this nectar and be happy.

एको विशुद्धबोधोऽहं इति निश्चयवह्निना।
प्रज्वाल्याज्ञानगहनं वीतशोकः सुखी भव ॥१-९॥

eko vishuddha bodha aham iti nishchaya vahinana |
prajvalya agyana gahanam vitashokah sukhi bhava ||1-9||

Firmly bearing the resolution "I am singular, pure consciousness" illuminates even the dense forest of ignorance. Be beyond grief, be happy.

यत्र विश्वमिदं भाति कल्पितं रज्जुसर्पवत्।
आनंदपरमानन्दः स बोधस्त्वं सुखं चर ॥१-१०॥

yatra vishvamidam bhati kalpitam rajjusarpavat |
anandaparamanandah sa bodhastvam sukham chara ||1-10||

Know and experience that joy and supreme bliss, wherein the world appears imaginary, like a snake imagined in a rope, and exist happily.

मुक्ताभिमानी मुक्तो हि बद्धो बद्धाभिमान्यपि।
किंवदन्तीह सत्येयं या मतिः सा गतिर्भवेत् ॥१-११॥

muktabhimani mukto hi baddho baddha abhimanyapi |
kivadantiham satyeyam ya matih sa gatirbhavet ||1-11||

If you think you are free, you are free and if you think you are bound, you are bound. It is rightly said "You become what you think."

आत्मा साक्षी विभुः पूर्ण एको मुक्तश्चिदक्रियः।
असंगो निःस्पृहः शान्तो भ्रमात्संसारवानिव ॥१-१२॥

atma sakshi vibhuh purna eko muktaschidakriyah |
asango nih spruhah shanto bhramat sansaravaniva ||1-12||

The Self is the witness. It is all-pervading, complete, singular, free, non-choosing, non-doing, unattached, desireless, completely peaceful. The world is merely an illusion, a projection.

ASHTAVAKRA GITA

कूटस्थं बोधमद्वैत- मात्मानं परिभावय।
आभासोऽहं भ्रमं मुक्त्वा भावं बाह्यमथान्तरम् ॥१-१३॥

kutastham bodhamadvaita matmanam paribhavaya |
abhasa aham bhramam muktva bhavam bahyam athantaram ||1-13||

Contemplate on the unchanging, non-dual consciousness that is the Self. The perception of "I" is a mere illusion – be free of it and feel the external as but a churning of the internal.

देहाभिमानपाशेन चिरं बद्धोऽसि पुत्रक।
बोधोऽहं ज्ञानखंगेन तन्निष्कृत्य सुखी भव ॥१-१४॥

deha abhimanapashena chiram baddho asi putraka |
bodho aham gnanakhangena tad nishkrutya sukhi bhava ||1-14||

O son, you have long been bound by the perception "I am the body". Realize the Self, and with that sword of knowledge, destroy that bondage and be happy.

निःसंगो निष्क्रियोऽसि त्वं स्वप्रकाशो निरंजनः।
अयमेव हि ते बन्धः समाधिमनुतिष्ठति ॥१-१५॥

nih sango nishkriyo asi tvam svaprakasho niranjanah |
ayameva hi te bandhah samadhim anutishthati ||1-15||

You are already unattached, non-doing, self-luminous and stainless. Practicing meditation (to achieve all this) is your bondage.

त्वया व्याप्तमिदं विश्वं त्वयि प्रोतं यथार्थतः।
शुद्धबुद्धस्वरूपस्त्वं मा गमः क्षुद्रचित्तताम् ॥१-१६॥

tvaya vyaptam idam vishvam tvayi protam yatharthah |
shuddha buddha svarupastvam ma gamah kshudrachit tatam ||1-16||

The entire universe is pervaded by you – indeed, it is all strung on you. You are a phenomenon of pure consciousness, do not be small-minded.

निरपेक्षो निर्विकारो निर्भरः शीतलाशयः।
अगाधबुद्धिरक्षुब्धो भव चिन्मात्रवासनः ॥१-१७॥

nirapeksho nirvikaro nirbharah shitalashayah |
agadha buddhih akshubdho bhava chinmatravasanah ||1-17||

You are unconditioned, changeless, abundant, a sanctuary of calmness, unfathomably intelligent, serene. Desire nothing but consciousness.

साकारमनृतं विद्धि निराकारं तु निश्चलं।
एतत्तत्त्वोपदेशेन न पुनर्भवसंभवः ॥१-१८॥

sakaram anrutam viddhi nirakaram tu nischalam |
etad tattva upadeshena na punarbhava sambhavah ||1-18||

Know that which has form is unreal, only the formless is permanent. Once you realize this teaching, you will not return again.

यथैवादर्शमध्यस्थे रूपेऽन्तः परितस्तु सः।
तथैवाऽस्मिन् शरीरेऽन्तः परितः परमेश्वरः ॥१-१९॥

yathaiva adarsham adhyasthe rupe antah paritastu sah |
tathaiva asmin sharire antah paritah parameshvarah ||1-19||

Just as a mirror exists in the middle of, inside of, and everywhere surrounding the image reflected, the Supreme Self exists inside of and everywhere surrounding the body.

एकं सर्वगतं व्योम बहिरन्तर्यथा घटे।
नित्यं निरन्तरं ब्रह्म सर्वभूतगणे तथा ॥१-२०॥

ekam sarvagatam vyoma bahir antaryatha ghate |
nityam nirantaram brahma sarvabhutagane tatha ||1-20||

Just as one all-pervading space exists both within and without a jar, so is the eternal, timeless Absolute in all.

TRANSLATED BY JANKI PARIKH

Chapter 2

जनक उवाच -
अहो निरंजनः शान्तो बोधोऽहं प्रकृतेः परः।
एतावंतमहं कालं मोहेनैव विडम्बितः ॥२-१॥

janaka uvacha
aho niranjanah shanto bodha aham prakruteh parah |
etavantam aham kalam mohenaiva vidambitah ||2-1||

Janaka said:
Indeed! I am flawless, peaceful, above nature, I am consciousness itself. How is it that all this time I was so deceived by delusion?

यथा प्रकाशयाम्येको देहमेनो तथा जगत्।
अतो मम जगत्सर्वमथवा न च किंचन ॥२-२॥

yatha prakashayamyeko deham eno tatha jagat |
ato mama jagat sarvam athava na cha kinchana ||2-2||

Just as I illuminate this one body, so I illuminate the world. Therefore, either the entire world is mine, or nothing is!

सशरीरमहो विश्वं परित्यज्य मयाऽधुना।
कुतश्चित् कौशलादेव परमात्मा विलोक्यते ॥२-३॥

sashariram aho vishvam parityajya maya adhuna |
kutaschit kaushaladeva paramatma vilokyate ||2-3||

Now, I renounce this body as well as this world. What a glorious experience this is, where even a non-divine person can see the Supreme Self!

यथा न तोयतो भिन्नास्तरंगाः फेन बुदबुदाः।
आत्मनो न तथा भिन्नं विश्वमात्मविनिर्गतम् ॥२-४॥

yatha na toyato bhinnastarangah fena budbudah |
atmano na tatha bhinnam vishvam atma vinirgatam ||2-4||

Just as waves, foam and bubbles are not different from water, so the universe emanating from the Self is not different from the Self.

तंतुमात्रो भवेदेव पटो यद्वद्विचारितः।
आत्मतन्मात्रमेवेदं तद्वद्विश्वं विचारितम् ॥२-५॥

tantumatro bhavedeva pato yadvad vicharitah |
atmatanmatram evedam tadvad vishvam vicharitam ||2-5||

When you think about it, cloth is merely thread. Similarly, when you think about it, the universe is merely an element of the Self.

यथैवेक्षुरसे क्लृप्ता तेन व्याप्तैव शर्करा।
तथा विश्वं मयि क्लृप्तं मया व्याप्तं निरन्तरम् ॥२-६॥

yathaiva akshurase klrupta tena vyaptaiva sharkara |
tatha vishvam mayi klruptam maya vyaptam nirantaram ||2-6||

Just as the sugar produced from sugarcane is pervaded by its flavour, so the universe emanating from me is endlessly pervaded by me.

आत्माऽज्ञानाज्जगद्भाति आत्मज्ञानान्न भासते।
रज्जवज्ञानादहिर्भाति तज्ज्ञानाद्भासते न हि ॥२-७॥

atma agyanat jagadbhati atmagyanat na bhasate |
rajjava gyanad ahirbhati tat gyanad bhasate na hi ||2-7||

When one is ignorant, a rope appears to be a snake; on realizing the truth, the snake does not appear any longer. Similarly, when one is ignorant of the Self, the world is seen; on realization of the Self, the world is no longer seen.

प्रकाशो मे निजं रूपं नातिरिक्तोऽस्म्यहं ततः।
यदा प्रकाशते विश्वं तदाऽहंभास एव हि ॥२-८॥

prakasho me nijam rupam natirikto asmyaham tatah |
yada prakashate vishvam tada ahambhasa eva hi ||2-8||

Light is my very essence – I am nothing other than that. Just as that light illuminates the world, so it also illuminates the perception of "I".

अहो विकल्पितं विश्वंज्ञानान्मयि भासते।
रूप्यं शुक्तौ फणी रज्जौ वारि सूर्यकरे यथा ॥२-९॥

aho vikalpitam vishvamgyananmayi bhasate |
rupyam shuktau fani rajjau vari suryakare yatha ||2-9||

Indeed! The imaginary universe appears in me because of ignorance, just as imaginary silver in mother-of-pearl, an imaginary snake in a rope, imaginary water in fierce sunlight (mirage).

मत्तो विनिर्गतं विश्वं मय्येव लयमेष्यति।
मृदि कुम्भो जले वीचिः कनके कटकं यथा ॥२-१०॥

mato vinirgatam vishvam mayi eva layam eshyati |
mrudi kumbho jale vichih kanake katakam yatha ||2-10||

The universe originates from me and is absorbed back into me, like a pot into clay, a wave into water, and a bangle into gold.

अहो अहं नमो मह्यं विनाशो यस्य नास्ति मे।
ब्रह्मादिस्तंबपर्यन्तं जगन्नाशोऽपि तिष्ठतः ॥२-११॥

aho aham namo mahyam vinasho yasya nasti me |
brahmadistamba paryantam jagat nasha api tishthatah ||2-11||

Indeed! I bow to my Self, which can never be destroyed! The Self stands even after the whole world is destroyed, from Brahma to the last blade of grass!

अहो अहं नमो मह्यं एकोऽहं देहवानपि।
क्वचिन्न गन्ता नागन्ता व्याप्य विश्वमवस्थितः ॥२-१२॥

aho aham namo mahyam eka aham dehavanapi |
kvachinna ganta naganta vyapya vishvam avasthitah ||2-12||

Indeed! I bow to my singular Self, who has a body, who does not go or come anywhere, yet stands pervading the entire universe.

अहो अहं नमो मह्यं दक्षो नास्तीह मत्समः।
असंस्पृश्य शरीरेण येन विश्वं चिरं धृतम् ॥२-१३॥

aho aham namo mahyam daksho nastiha matsamah |
asamsprushya sharirena yena vishvam chiram dhrutam ||2-13||

Indeed! I bow to my wise Self - there is nobody equal to me, who without touching the body, holds the entire universe!

अहो अहं नमो मह्यं यस्य मे नास्ति किंचन।
अथवा यस्य मे सर्वं यद्वाङ्मनसगोचरम् ॥२-१४॥

aho aham namo mahyam yasya me nasti kinchana |
athava yasya me sarvam yadvan manasa gocharam ||2-14||

Indeed! I bow to my Self, who owns nothing, or else owns everything that can be perceived by the mind.

ज्ञानं ज्ञेयं तथा ज्ञाता त्रितयं नास्ति वास्तवं।
अज्ञानाद् भाति यत्रेदं सोऽहमस्मि निरंजनः ॥२-१५॥

gyanam gyeyam tatha tritayam nasti vastavam |
agyanad bhati yatredam soham asmi niranjanah ||2-15||

Knowledge, the known, the knower, all three do not exist in reality. The Self is flawless, and appears as these three due to lack of awareness.

द्वैतमूलमहो दुःखं नान्यत्तस्यास्ति भेषजं।
दृश्यमेतन् मृषा सर्वं एकोऽहं चिद्रसोमलः ॥२-१६॥

dvaitamulamaho dukham na anyat tasya asti bheshajam |
drashyam etan mrusha sarvam eka aham chidrasomalah ||2-16||

Indeed, duality is the root cause of suffering. There is no remedy for it, other than knowing that whatever is visible is unreal, and that I am one, pure consciousness.

बोधमात्रोऽहमज्ञानाद् उपाधिः कल्पितो मया।
एवं विमृशतो नित्यं निर्विकल्पे स्थितिर्मम ॥२-१७॥

bodhamatra aham agyanad upadhih kalpito maya |
evam vimrushato nityam nirvikalpe sthitirmama ||2-17||

I am only the final apex of higher knowledge, all other attributes of mine are imaginary. Contemplating this constantly, I stand unwavering.

न मे बन्धोऽस्ति मोक्षो वा भ्रान्तिः शान्तो निराश्रया।
अहो मयि स्थितं विश्वं वस्तुतो न मयि स्थितम् ॥२-१८॥

na me bandho asti moksho va bhrantih shanto nirashraya |
aho mayi sthitam vishvam vastuto na mayi sthitam ||2-18||

Neither bondage nor liberation quiver inside me. I am calm, needing no refuge. Indeed! This universe, though standing in me, in reality does not exist in me.

सशरीरमिदं विश्वं न किंचिदिति निश्चितं।
शुद्धचिन्मात्र आत्मा च तत्कस्मिन् कल्पनाधुना ॥२-१९॥

sashariram idam vishvam na kinchit iti nishchitam |
shuddha chinmatra atma cha tatkasmin kalpanadhuna ||2-19||

Definitely, this body and this world are nothing. Only pure, conscious Self exists. Now what else is there to imagine?

शरीरं स्वर्गनरकौ बन्धमोक्षौ भयं तथा।
कल्पनामात्रमेवैतत् किं मे कार्यं चिदात्मनः ॥२-२०॥

shariram svargan arakau bandhamokshau bhayam tatha |
kalpanamatram evaitat kim me karyam chidatmanah ||2-20||

The body, heaven, hell, bondage, liberation and fear, all these are imaginary. What use are these to the conscious Self?

अहो जनसमूहेऽपि न द्वैतं पश्यतो मम।
अरण्यमिव संवृत्तं क्व रतिं करवाण्यहम् ॥२-२१॥

aho janasamuhe api na dvaitam pashyato mama |
aranyam iva samvruttam kva ratim karavani aham ||2-21||

Indeed, I do not see duality even in a crowd of people, everything appears covered by the desert. What is there to be enamoured of?

नाहं देहो न मे देहो जीवो नाहमहं हि चित्।
अयमेव हि मे बन्ध आसीद्या जीविते स्पृहा ॥२-२२॥

naham deho na me deho jivo naham aham hi chit |
ayam eva hi me bandha asidya jivite spruha ||2-22||

I am not the body, nor is the body mine. I am not this life, I am only consciousness. My only bondage is the thirst for life.

अहो भुवनकल्लोलैर्विचित्रैर्द्राक् समुत्थितं।
मय्यनंतमहांभोधौ चित्तवाते समुद्यते ॥२-२३॥

aho bhuvan akallolaih vichitrairdrak samutthitam |
mayi ananta mahambhodhau chittavate samudyate ||2-23||

Indeed! When the great, infinite ocean of myself experiences joy, waves of strange worlds are awakened and stirred up!

मय्यनंतमहांभोधौ चित्तवाते प्रशाम्यति।
अभाग्याज्जीववणिजो जगत्पोतो विनश्वरः ॥२-२४॥

mayi ananta mahambhodhau chittavate prashamyati |
abhagyat jivavanijo jagatpoto vinashvarah ||2-24||

And when the great, infinite ocean of myself experiences calmness, the worlds are destroyed, like misfortunate traders on a boat in the ocean.

मय्यनन्तमहांभोधा-वाश्चर्यं जीववीचयः।
उद्यन्ति घ्नन्ति खेलन्ति प्रविशन्ति स्वभावतः ॥२-२५॥

mayi ananta mahambhodha vashcharyam jivavichayah |
udyanti ghnanti khelanti pravishanti svabhavatah ||2-25||

It's amazing! In the great, infinite ocean of myself, constellations of existences naturally arise, multiply, play, and go back to source.

Chapter 3

अष्टावक्र उवाच -
अविनाशिनमात्मानं एकं विज्ञाय तत्त्वतः।
तवात्मज्ञानस्य धीरस्य कथमर्थार्जने रतिः ॥३-१॥

ashtavakra uvacha
avinashinam atmanam ekam vigyaya tattvatah |
tavatmagyanasya dhirasya katham artharjane ratih ||3-1||

Ashtavakra said –
Know the truth - the Self is indestructible and one. With that self-knowledge, how can the wise one be attracted to achieving wealth?

आत्मज्ञानादहो प्रीतिर्विषयभ्रमगोचरे।
शुक्तेरज्ञानतो लोभो यथा रजतविभ्रमे ॥३-२॥

atmagyanad aho pritirvishaya bhramagochare |
shukteragyanato lobho yatha rajatavibhrame ||3-2||

Ignorance about the Self leads to a deluded attachment to sense objects, just as ignorance about mother-of-pearl leads to greed and delusion that it is silver.

विश्वं स्फुरति यत्रेदं तरङ्गा इव सागरे।
सोऽहमस्मीति विज्ञाय किं दीन इव धावसि ॥३-३॥

vishvam sfurati yatredam taranga iva sagare |
soham asmi iti vigyaya kim dina iva dhavasi ||3-3||

After recognizing 'I am that from whom the universe springs like waves from the sea', why run around so pitifully?

श्रुत्वापि शुद्धचैतन्य आत्मानमतिसुन्दरं।
उपस्थेऽत्यन्तसंसक्तो मालिन्यमधिगच्छति ॥३-४॥

shrutva api shuddha chaitanya atmanam atisundaram |
upasthe atyantasansakto malinyam adhigachhati ||3-4||

After hearing that the Self is pure consciousness and extremely beautiful, why approach impurities, and be so closely attached to and worship them?

सर्वभूतेषु चात्मानं सर्वभूतानि चात्मनि।
मुनेर्जानत आश्चर्यं ममत्वमनुवर्तते ॥३-५॥

sarvabhuteshu cha atmanam sarvabhutani cha atmani |
munerjanata ashcharyam mamatvam anuvartate ||3-5||

For a sage who knows that the Self is in all beings, and all beings are in the Self, practicing "I-ness" is surprising!

आस्थितः परमाद्वैतं मोक्षार्थेऽपि व्यवस्थितः।
आश्चर्यं कामवशगो विकलः केलिशिक्षया ॥३-६॥

asthitah paramadvaitam moksharthe api vyavasthitah |
ashcharyam kamavashago vikalah kelishikshaya ||3-6||

It is surprising indeed that the one existing for and aspiring to liberation through supreme non-duality should be defeated by the twisted skillful play of lust! ||3-6||

उद्भूतं ज्ञानदुर्मित्रम्-वधार्यातिदुर्बलः।
आश्चर्यं काममाकाङ्क्षेत् कालमन्तमनुश्रितः ॥3-7॥

adbhutam gyanadurmitram vadharyati durbalah |
ashcharyam kamam akankshet kalam antamanushritah ||3-7||

The animal of lust is the enemy of knowledge, and is like a thunderbolt making you exceedingly weak. It is astonishing indeed to let it take possession of you and obey it right up to the end of time!

इहामुत्र विरक्तस्य नित्यानित्यविवेकिनः।
आश्चर्यं मोक्षकामस्य मोक्षाद् एव विभीषिका ॥3-8॥

ihamutra viraktasya nitya anitya vivekinah |
ashcharyam mokshakamasya moksha deva vibhishika ||3-8||

It is astonishing that those who are indifferent to this world and the next, who are aware of the difference between the permanent and the impermanent, who desire liberation, are terrified of liberation! ||3-8||

धीरस्तु भोज्यमानोऽपि पीड्यमानोऽपि सर्वदा।
आत्मानं केवलं पश्यन् न तुष्यति न कुप्यति ॥3-9॥

dhirastu bhojyamana api pidyamana api sarvada |
atmanam kevalam pashyan na tushyati na kupyati ||3-9||

The wise who always perceive the Self only, are neither satisfied nor angry whether they are celebrated or censured.

चेष्टमानं शरीरं स्वं पश्यत्यन्यशरीरवत्।
संस्तवे चापि निन्दायां कथं क्षुभ्येत् महाशयः ॥३-१०॥

cheshtamanam shariram svam pashyati anya shariravat |
sanstave cha api nindayam katham kshubhyet mahashayah ||3-10||

How can praise or blame disturb the great noble soul who is inclined towards seeing one's own body in other bodies?

मायामात्रमिदं विश्वं पश्यन् विगतकौतुकः।
अपि सन्निहिते मृत्यौ कथं त्रस्यति धीरधीः ॥३-११॥

mayamatram idam vishvam pashyan vigatakautukah |
api sannihite mrutyau katham trasyati dhiradhih ||3-11||

How can the great, wise one who is without curiosity, who perceives this world as merely maya, quake with fear when close to death?

निःस्पृहं मानसं यस्य नैराश्येऽपि महात्मनः।
तस्यात्मज्ञानतृप्तस्य तुलना केन जायते ॥३-१२॥

nih spruham manasam yasya nairashye api mahatmanah |
tasyatmagyana truptasya tulana kena jayate ||3-12||

Who can be compared to the great soul whose mind is desireless even in disappointment, and who is completely content in the knowledge of the self?

भावाद् एव जानानो दृश्यमेतन्न किंचन।
इदं ग्राह्यमिदं त्याज्यं स किं पश्यति धीरधीः ॥३-१३॥

svabhavad eva janano drashyam etad na kinchana |
idam grahyam idam tyajyam sa kim pashyati dhiradhih ||3-13||

Know all this that is seen is, by its very nature, nothing. Then how can the wise one think 'I accept this' or 'I reject this'?

अंतस्त्यक्तकषायस्य निर्द्वन्द्वस्य निराशिषः।
यदृच्छयागतो भोगो न दुःखाय न तुष्टये ॥३-१४॥

antastyaktakashayasya nirdvandvasya nirashishah |
yadrat shayagato bhogo na dukhaya na tushtaye ||3-14||

The one who has given up intense desires, who is without doubts and without blessings, is neither sorrowful nor pleased on experiencing random events.

Chapter 4

अष्टावक्र उवाच -
हन्तात्मज्ञस्य धीरस्य खेलतो भोगलीलया।
न हि संसारवाहीकैर्मूढैः सह समानता ॥४-१॥

ashtavakra uvacha
hantatmagyasya dhirasya khelato bhogalilaya |
na hi sansaravahikairmudhaih saha samanata ||4-1||

Ashtavakra said –
Indeed! The self-knowing wise one plays when he experiences leela. He cannot be compared to the fool who carries the world upon his shoulders.

यत् पदं प्रेप्सवो दीनाः शक्राद्याः सर्वदेवताः।
अहो तत्र स्थितो योगी न हर्षमुपगच्छति ॥४-२॥

yat padam prepsavo Dinah shakradyah sarvadevatah |
aho tatra sthito yogi na harsham upagachhati ||4-2||

Indeed! Even on attaining the state that Indra and all gods crave, the yogi does not go into ecstasies.

तज्ज्ञस्य पुण्यपापाभ्यां स्पर्शो ह्यन्तर्न जायते।
न ह्याकाशस्य धूमेन दृश्यमानापि सङ्गतिः ॥४-३॥

tat gyasya punyapapabhyam sparsho hi antarna jayate |
na hyakashasya dhumena drashyamanapi sangatih ||4-3||

The one with this knowledge remains untouched internally by good or bad, just as the sky, even when perceiving smoke, is untouched by it.

आत्मैवेदं जगत्सर्वं ज्ञातं येन महात्मना।
यदृच्छया वर्तमानं तं निषेद्धुं क्षमेत कः ॥४-४॥

atmai vedam jagatsarvam gyatam yena mahatmana |
yadrat shaya vartamanam tam nisheddhum kshameta kah ||4-4||

Who can hold back the great soul who knows the whole world as Self, from existing in the present as per his own wish?

आब्रह्मस्तंबपर्यन्ते भूतग्रामे चतुर्विधे।
विज्ञस्यैव हि सामर्थ्यमिच्छानिच्छाविवर्जने ॥४-५॥

abrahmastamba paryante bhutagrame chaturvidhe |
vigyasyaiva hi samarthyam ichhan ichhavivarjane ||4-5||

From Brahma to a blade of grass, amongst all four categories of living beings, only the enlightened one is powerful enough to give up all desires and aversions.

आत्मानमद्वयं कश्चिज्जानाति जगदीश्वरं।
यद् वेत्ति तत्स कुरुते न भयं तस्य कुत्रचित् ॥४-६॥

atmanam advayam kashchid janati jagadishvaram |
yad vetti tatsa kurute na bhayam tasya kutrachit ||4-6||

Rare are those who know the Self as the non-dual lord of the world! Those who know this do not fear anything anywhere.

Chapter 5

अष्टावक्र उवाच –
न ते संगोऽस्ति केनापि किं शुद्धस्त्यक्तुमिच्छसि।
संघातविलयं कुर्वन्नेवमेव लयं व्रज ॥५- १॥

ashtavakra uvacha
na te sangasti kenapi kim shuddhastyaktum ichhasi |
sanghatavilayam kurvannevam eva layam vraja ||5-1||

Ashtavakra said –
You are not attached to anything. You are extremely pure, what do you wish to renounce? Dissolve this connection and roam carefree!

उदेति भवतो विश्वं वारिधेरिव बुद्बुदः।
इति ज्ञात्वैकमात्मानं एवमेव लयं व्रज ॥५- २॥

udeti bhavato vishvam varidheriva budbudah |
iti gyatvaikam atmanam evameva layam vraja ||5-2||

The universe arises from the non-dual Self like bubbles arise from the sea. Knowing this, roam carefree!

प्रत्यक्षमप्यवस्तुत्वाद् विश्वं नास्त्यमले त्वयि।
रज्जुसर्प इव व्यक्तं एवमेव लयं व्रज ॥५- ३॥

pratyaksham apyavastutvad vishvam nastyamale tvayi |
rajjusarpa iva vyaktam evameva layam vraja ||5-3||

Just as a snake is visible in a rope, the universe is manifest right before you, but does not really exist in you, who are completely pure. Therefore, roam carefree!

समदुःखसुखः पूर्ण आशानैराश्यययोः समः।
समजीवितमृत्युः सन्नेवमेव लयं व्रज ॥५-४॥

sama dukkha sukha purna ashanairashyayoh samah |
samajivitamrutyuh sannevameva layam vraja ||5-4||

Know yourself the same in happiness or sorrow, complete, equanimous in hope and disappointment, equanimous in life and death, and eternal. Thus, roam carefree!

Chapter 6

अष्टावक्र उवाच –
आकाशवदनन्तोऽहं घटवत् प्राकृतं जगत्।
इति ज्ञानं तथैतस्य न त्यागो न ग्रहो लयः ॥६-१॥

ashtavakra uvacha
akashavadananta aham ghatavat prakrutam jagat |
iti gyanam tathaitasya na tyago na graho layah ||6-1||

Ashtavakra said –
"I am infinite like space, and the world is ordinary like a jar." This is knowledge. Do not renounce or accept it, just dissolve into it.

महोदधिरिवाहं स प्रपंचो वीचिसऽन्निभः।
इति ज्ञानं तथैतस्य न त्यागो न ग्रहो लयः ॥६-२॥

mahod adhirivaham sa prapancho vichisa annibhah |
iti gyanam tathaitasya na tyago na graho layah ||6-2||

"I am like a vast ocean and this entire creation is like its waves." This is knowledge. Do not renounce or accept it, just dissolve into it.

अहं स शुक्तिसङ्काशो रूप्यवद् विश्वकल्पना।
इति ज्ञानं तथैतस्य न त्यागो न ग्रहो लयः ॥६-३॥

aham sa shukti sankasho rupyavad vishvakalpana |
iti gyanam tathaitasya na tyago na graho layah ||6-3||

"I am like mother-of-pearl and this universe is imagined in me like silver." This is knowledge. Do not renounce or accept it, just dissolve into it.

अहं वा सर्वभूतेषु सर्वभूतान्यथो मयि।
इति ज्ञानं तथैतस्य न त्यागो न ग्रहो लयः ॥६-४॥

aham va sarvabhuteshu sarvabhutan yatho mayi |
iti gyanam tathaitasya na tyago na graho layah ||6-4||

"I am in every being and every being is in me." This is knowledge. Do not renounce or accept it, just dissolve into it.

Chapter 7

जनक उवाच -
मय्यनंतमहांभोधौ विश्वपोत इतस्ततः ।
भ्रमति स्वांतवातेन न ममास्त्यसहिष्णुता ॥७-१॥

janaka uvacha
mayi anantamahambhodhau vishvapota itastatah |
bhramati svantavatena na mamastya sahishnuta ||7-1||

Janaka said –
In the great infinite ocean of my Self, the universe wanders here and there like a ship directed by its own wind, but it does not cause any disturbance in me.

मय्यनंतमहांभोधौ जगद्वीचिः स्वभावतः ।
उदेतु वास्तमायातु न मे वृद्धिर्न च क्षतिः ॥७-२॥

mayi anantamahambhodhau jagadvichih svabhavatah |
udetu vastamayatu na me vruddhirna cha kshatih ||7-2||

In the great infinite ocean of my Self, the wave of the universe naturally rises and falls, but does not cause any increase or decrease in me.

मय्यनंतमहांभोधौ विश्वं नाम विकल्पना ।
अतिशांतो निराकार एतदेवाहमास्थितः ॥७-३॥

mayi anantamahambhodhau vishvam nama vikalpana |
atishanto nirakara etad evaham asthitah ||7-3||

In the great infinite ocean of my Self, there is an imaginative creation called the universe. But I stand exactly as I am - supremely peaceful and beyond all forms!

नात्मा भावेषु नो भावस्तत्रानन्ते निरंजने।
इत्यसक्तोऽस्पृहः शान्त एतदेवाहमास्थितः ॥७-४॥

na atma bhaveshu no bhavastatra anante niranjane |
ityasakto aspruhah shanta etad evaham asthitah ||7-4||

The Self is not born of any emotion, nor does it possess any emotion. In that infinite and stainless state I stand as I am - unattached, desireless and peaceful!

अहो चिन्मात्रमेवाहं इन्द्रजालोपमं जगत्।
अतो मम कथं कुत्र हेयोपादेयकल्पना ॥७-५॥

aho chinmatram evaham indrajalopamam jagat |
ato mama katham kurta heyopadeya Kalpana ||7-5||

Indeed! I am pure consciousness, and the world is like a web of illusion. Then how and from where can thoughts of glory or disgrace arise in me?

Chapter 8

अष्टावक्र उवाच -
तदा बन्धो यदा चित्तं किन्चिद् वांछति शोचति।
किंचिन् मुंचति गृण्हाति किंचिद् हृष्यति कुप्यति ॥८-१॥

ashtavakra uvacha
tada bandho yada chittam kinchid vanchhati shochati |
kinchin munchati grunhati kinchid hrushyati kupyati ||8-1||

Ashtavakra said:
There is bondage when the mind craves or grieves for something, sacrifices or grabs something, is pleased or angry about something.

तदा मुक्तिर्यदा चित्तं न वांछति न शोचति।
न मुंचति न गृण्हाति न हृष्यति न कुप्यति ॥८- २॥

tada mukriryada chittam na vanchhati na shochati |
na munchati na grunhati na hrushyati na kupyati ||8-2||

It is liberation when the mind neither craves nor grieves, neither gives up nor grabs, is neither pleased nor angry.

तदा बन्धो यदा चित्तं सक्तं काश्वपि दृष्टिषु।
तदा मोक्षो यदा चित्तम्-सक्तं सर्वदृष्टिषु ॥८- ३॥

tada bandho yada chittam saktam kashvapi drashtishu |
tada moksho yada chittam saktam sarvadrashtishu ||8-3||

There is bondage when the mind is attached to shiny visible objects. It is liberation when the mind is not attached to anything visible.

यदा नाहं तदा मोक्षो यदाहं बन्धनं तदा।
मत्वेति हेलया किंचिन्-मा गृहाण विमुंच मा ॥८-४॥

yada naham tada moksho yadaham bandhanam tada |
matveti helaya kinchin ma gruhana vimuncha ma ||8-4||

Where there is no "I", there is liberation; where there is "I", there is bondage. Knowing this, be relaxed - neither grab on to nor sacrifice anything.

Chapter 9

अष्टावक्र उवाच -
कृताकृते च द्वन्द्वानि कदा शान्तानि कस्य वा।
एवं ज्ञात्वेह निर्वेदाद् भवत्यागपरोऽव्रती ॥९-१॥

ashtavakra uvacha
krutakrute cha dvandvani kada shantani kasya va |
evam gyatveha nirvedad bhava tyagaparo avrati ||9-1||

Ashtavakra said –
What is to be done and what is not to be done are dualities that have never subsided in anybody. Knowing this, be neutral, renounce the world, and be above rituals.

कस्यापि तात धन्यस्य लोकचेष्टावलोकनात्।
जीवितेच्छा बुभुक्षा च बुभुत्सोपशमं गताः ॥९-२॥

kasyapi tata dhanyasya lokacheshtavalokanat |
jivitechha bubhuksha cha bubhutsopashamam gatah ||9-2||

Blessed are those who behold the endeavours of others, and thereby extinguish their own desire, lust and hunger for life!

नित्यं सर्वमेवेदं तापत्रयदूषितं।
असारं निन्दितं हेयमिति निश्चित्य शाम्यति ॥९-३॥

nityam sarvam evedam tapatrayadushitam |
asaram nindatam heyam iti nischitya shamyati ||9-3||

All this (the world) is impermanent and is polluted by three types of pain. It is without any moral conclusion, contemptible and is to be abandoned. After deciding this, there is peace.

कोऽसौ कालो वयः किं वा यत्र द्वन्द्वानि नो नृणाम्।
तान्युपेक्ष्य यथाप्राप्तवर्ती सिद्धिमवाप्नुयात् ॥९-४॥

ko asau kalo vayah kim va yatra dvandvani no nrunam |
tanyupekshya yatha praptavarti siddhim avapnuyat ||9-4||

Was there ever a time when people did not experience dualities? So be without expectations, be as you are, and reach the highest goal naturally.

नाना मतं महर्षीणां साधूनां योगिनां तथा।
दृष्ट्वा निर्वेदमापन्नः को न शाम्यति मानवः ॥९-५॥

nana matam maharshinam sadhunam yoginam tatha |
drashtva nirvedam apannah ko na shamyati manavah ||9-5||

Seeing the diverse opinions of great people, sages and yogis, which person will not become indifferent and achieve peace?

कृत्वा मूर्तिपरिज्ञानं चैतन्यस्य न किं गुरुः।
निर्वेदसमतायुक्त्या यस्तारयति संसृतेः ॥९-६॥

krutva murti parigyanam chaitanyasya na kim guruh |
nirveda samatayuktya yastarayati sansruteh ||9-6||

Realizing higher knowledge beyond idol worship, which guru's consciousness will not be awakened? The one who is indifferent, who is equanimously established saves this entire creation!

पश्य भूतविकारांस्त्वं भूतमात्रान् यथार्थतः।
तत्क्षणाद् बन्धनिर्मुक्तः स्वरूपस्थो भविष्यसि ॥९-७॥

pashya bhutavikaranstvam bhutamatran yatharthatah |
tatkshanad bandhanirmuktah svarupastho bhavishyasi ||9-7||

See the changes in existence as intrinsically subtle elements of existence. In that very instance, be free from bondage and be established in your own nature.

वासना एव संसार इति सर्वा विमुंच ताः।
तत्त्यागो वासनात्यागात्स्थितिरद्य यथा तथा ॥९-८॥

vasana eva samsara iti sarva vimuncha tah |
tattyago vasanatyagat sthitiradya yatha tatha ||9-8||

Desire itself is the world – therefore, renounce it all. Renouncing the world means renouncing desire, and being steady exactly as you are.

Chapter 10

अष्टावक्र उवाच -
विहाय वैरिणं कामम-र्थं चानर्थसंकुलं।
धर्ममप्येतयोर्हेतुं सर्वत्रानादरं कुरु ॥१०-१॥

ashtavakra uvacha
vihaya vairinam kamam artham cha anarthasankulam |
dharmam apyetayorhetum sarvatra anadaram kuru ||10-1||

Ashtavakra said –
Abandon the enemies of lust and wealth, which cause confusion and misfortunes. For reaching righteousness, be indifferent to everything.

स्वप्नेन्द्रजालवत् पश्य दिनानि त्रीणि पंच वा।
मित्रक्षेत्रधनागार-दारदायादिसंपदः ॥१०-२॥

svapna indrajalavat pashya dinani trini pancha va |
mitrakshetradhanagara daradayadi sampadah ||10-2||

See friends, land, money, house, an ocean of wealth and all that like a web of dreams, existing only for three to five days.

यत्र भवेतृष्णा संसारं विद्धि तत्र वै।
प्रौढवैराग्यमाश्रित्य वीततृष्णः सुखी भव ॥१०-३॥

yatra bhavetrushna sansaram viddhi tatra vai |
praudha vairagyam ashritya vitatrushnah sukhi bhava ||10-3||

Know wherever there is ardent desire, there is the world! Taking refuge in this mature non-attachment, be without desire, and be happy!

तृष्णामात्रात्मको बन्धस्-तन्नाशो मोक्ष उच्यते।
भवासंसक्तिमात्रेण प्राप्तितुष्टिर्मुहुर्मुहुः ॥१०-४॥

trushnamatratmako bandhas tad nasho moksha uchyate |
bhavasansakti matrena prapti tushtir muhurmuhuh ||10-4||

Desire alone is the bondage of the self. Destroying desire is called liberation. Being unattached to objects of desire leads to contentment in every moment!

त्वमेकश्चेतनः शुद्धो जडं विश्वमसत्तथा।
अविद्यापि न किंचित्सा का बुभुत्सा तथापि ते ॥१०-५॥

tvam ekaschetanah shuddho jadam vishvamasat tatha |
avidyapi na kinchitsa ka bubhutsa tathapi te ||10-5||

You are one, pure consciousness, the world is non-conscious and unreal. You have neither the slightest ignorance nor any curiosity to know anything.

राज्यं सुताः कलत्राणि शरीराणि सुखानि च।
संसक्तस्यापि नष्टानि तव जन्मनि जन्मनि ॥१०-६॥

rajyam sutah kalatrani sharirani sukhani cha |
sansaktasyapi nashtani tava janmani janmani ||10-6||

Kingdoms, children, consorts, bodies, happiness, close attachments, all of these are destroyed, life after life.

अलमर्थेन कामेन सुकृतेनापि कर्मणा।
एभ्यः संसारकान्तारे न विश्रान्तमभून् मनः ॥१०-७॥

alam arthena kamena sukrutenapi karmana |
ebhyah sansara kantare na vishrantam abhun manah ||10-7||

Even great wealth, desire and good deeds will not result in rest for the mind from the disaster of this world.

कृतं न कति जन्मानि कायेन मनसा गिरा।
दुःखमायासदं कर्म तदद्याप्युपरम्यताम् ॥१०-८॥

krutam na kati janmani kayena manasa gira |
dukham ayasadam karma taddyapyuramyatam ||10-8||

Have you not spent various lives performing actions with the body, mind and speech, and incurring pain consistently? Now be above all these.

Chapter 11

अष्टावक्र उवाच –
भावाभावविकारश्च स्वभावादिति निश्चयी।
निर्विकारो गतक्लेशः सुखेनैवोपशाम्यति ॥११-१॥

ashtavakra uvacha
bhavabhava vikarashcha svabhavaditi nishchayi |
nirvikaro gatakleshah sukhenaiva upashamyati ||11-1||

Ashtavakra said –
"Transformations like being and non-being occur naturally." The one who knows this firmly becomes calm and happy, without disturbances and without worries.

ईश्वरः सर्वनिर्माता नेहान्य इति निश्चयी।
अन्तर्गलितसर्वाशः शान्तः क्वापि न सज्जते ॥११-२॥

ishvarah sarvanirmata nehanya iti nishchayi |
antargalita sarvashah shantah kvapi na sajjate ||11-2||

"The Supreme One is the creator of all, no one else is." The one who knows this firmly calms his all-consuming internal hunger, and not wandering anywhere, becomes steady.

आपदः संपदः काले दैवादेवेति निश्चयी।
तृप्तः स्वस्थेन्द्रियो नित्यं न वान्छति न शोचति ॥११-३॥

apadah sampadah kale daivadeveti nischayi |
truptah svastha indriyo nityam na vanchhati na shochati ||11-3||

"Misfortune and fortune are merely due to non-divine and divine times." The one who knows this firmly becomes content, with always steady senses, and neither desires nor get disappointed.

सुखदुःखे जन्ममृत्यू दैवादेवेति निश्चयी।
साध्यादर्शी निरायासः कुर्वन्नपि न लिप्यते ॥११-४॥

sukhdukhe janmamrutyu daivadeveti nishchayi |
sadhyadarshi nirayasah kurvannapi na lipyate ||11-4||

"Joy and sorrow, birth and death are of divine and non-divine origin." The one who knows this firmly sets his sights on the goal, and acts without desire, neither doing, nor getting attached.

चिन्तया जायते दुःखं नान्यथेहेति निश्चयी।
तया हीनः सुखी शान्तः सर्वत्र गलितस्पृहः ॥११-५॥

chintaya jayate dukham na anyatheheti nischayi |
taya hinah sukhi shantah sarvatra galitspruhah ||11-5||

"It is worry that gives birth to suffering, nothing else." The one who knows this firmly is free from worry, happy and calm, all longings having perished.

नाहं देहो न मे देहो बोधोऽहमिति निश्चयी।
कैवल्यं इव संप्राप्तो न स्मरत्यकृतं कृतम् ॥११-६॥

naham deho na me deho bodho aham iti nishchayi |
kaivalyam iva samprapto na smaratyakrutam krutam ||11-6||

"I am not the body, nor is this body mine. I am pure consciousness." The one who knows this firmly obtains emancipation, neither thinking about past acts, nor focusing on future actions.

आब्रह्मस्तंबपर्यन्तं अहमेवेति निश्चयी।
निर्विकल्पः शुचिः शान्तः प्राप्ताप्राप्तविनिर्वृतः ॥११-७॥

abrahmastambaparyantam aham eveti nishchayi |
nirvikalpah shuchih shantah prapta aprapta vinirvrutah ||11-7||

"From Brahma down to a clump of grass, I alone exist, and nothing else." The one who knows this firmly is without choice, pure, calm, and unattached to what he has or doesn't have.

नाश्चर्यमिदं विश्वं न किंचिदिति निश्चयी।
निर्वासनः स्फूर्तिमात्रो न किंचिदिव शाम्यति ॥११-८॥

nascharyam idam vishvam na kinchit iti nishchayi |
nirvasanah sfurtimatro na kinchit iva shamyati ||11-8||

"This astonishing universe is nothing." The one who knows this firmly is without fanciful imagination, is still with not even a vibration, is completely tranquil.

Chapter 12

जनक उवाच -
कायकृत्यासहः पूर्वं ततो वाग्विस्तरासहः।
अथ चिन्तासहस्तस्माद् एवमेवाहमास्थितः ॥१२-१॥

janaka uvacha
kayakrutyasahah purvam tato vagvistarasahah |
atha chintasahastasmad evam evaham asthitah ||12-1||

Janaka said –
First, I became indifferent to actions performed by the body. Then I became indifferent to the expanse of speech. Now I have become indifferent to all worries, and I stand exactly as I am!

प्रीत्यभावेन शब्दादेर-दृश्यत्वेन चात्मनः।
विक्षेपैकाग्रहृदय एवमेवाहमास्थितः ॥१२-२॥

prityabhavena shabdadera drashyatvena cha atmanah |
vikshepaikagrahrudaya evam evaham asthitah ||12-2||

The Self is not attached to pleasant feelings, sounds or sight. Unchained to disturbances, I stand exactly as I!

समाध्यासादिविक्षिप्तौ व्यवहारः समाधये।
एवं विलोक्य नियमं एवमेवाहमास्थितः ॥१२-३॥

samadhyasadivikshiptau vyavaharah samadhaye |
evam vilokya niyamam evam evaham asthitah ||12-3||

The non-meditative state and the meditative state keep moving back and forth (in the mind). Seeing this as a natural rule, I stand exactly as I am!

हेयोपादेयविरहाद् एवं हर्षविषादयोः।
अभावादद्य हे ब्रह्मन्न् एवमेवाहमास्थितः ॥१२-४॥

heyopadeya virahad evam harshavishadayoh |
abhavadadya he brahmana evamevaham asthitah ||12-4||

In a blank state of being, devoid of feelings of praise-censure and joy-sorrow, O Brahman, I stand exactly as I am!

आश्रमानाश्रमं ध्यानं चित्तस्वीकृतवर्जनं।
विकल्पं मम वीक्ष्यै-तैरेवमेवाहमास्थितः ॥१२-५॥

ashraman ashramam dhyanam chittasvikruta varjanam |
vikalpam mama vikshyai tairevam evaham asthitah ||12-5||

Recognizing that stages of life (Ashramas) or their absence, meditation, various things accepted or rejected by the mind are all my own wondrous projections, I stand exactly as I am!

कर्मानुष्ठानमज्ञानाद् यथैवोपरमस्तथा।
बुध्वा सम्यगिदं तत्त्वं एवमेवाहमास्थितः ॥१२-६॥

karman ushthanam agyanad yathaivoparamastatha |
budhva samyagidam tattvam evamevaham asthitah ||12-6||

Following rituals is ignorance; therefore, I am above that. Knowing the truth accurately, I stand exactly as I am!

अचिंत्यं चिंत्यमानोऽपि चिन्तारूपं भजत्यसौ।
त्यक्त्वा तद्भावनं तस्माद् एवमेवाहमास्थितः ॥१२-७॥

achintyam chintyamana api chintarupam bhajatyasau |
tyaktva tadbhavanam tasmad evam evaham asthitah ||12-7||

While contemplating the Inconceivable, it is only thoughts that we contemplate. Therefore, abandoning that state of mind, I stand exactly as I am!

एवमेव कृतं येन स कृतार्थो भवेदसौ।
एवमेव स्वभावो यः स कृतार्थो भवेदसौ ॥१२-८॥

evam eva krutam yena sa krutartho bhavedasau |
evameva svabhavo yah sa krutartho bhavedasau ||12-8||

One who acts like this is truly contented. One whose nature is like this is truly contented.

Chapter 13

जनक उवाच-
अकिंचनभवं स्वास्थ्यं कौपीनत्वेऽपि दुर्लभं।
त्यागादाने विहायास्मादहमासे यथासुखम् ॥१३-१॥

janaka uvacha
akinchanabhavam svasthyam kaupinatve api durlabham |
tyagadane vihaya asmad ahamase yatha sukham ||13-1||

Janaka said –
The state of nothingness is difficult to attain even if one wears just a loin-cloth. Therefore, I exist happily in every situation, without either renunciation or charity.

कुत्रापि खेदः कायस्य जिह्वा कुत्रापि खेद्यते।
मनः कुत्रापि तत्यक्त्वा पुरुषार्थे स्थितः सुखम् ॥१३-२॥

kutrapi khedah kayasya jihva kutrapi khedyate |
manah kutrapi tatyaktva purusharthe sthitah sukham ||13-2||

Truly, where is any pain because of the body, where is any pain because of the tongue, where is any pain because of the mind? Abandoning all effort, I exist happily.

कृतं किमपि नैवस्याद् इति संचिन्त्य तत्त्वतः।
यदा यत्कर्तुमायाति तत् कृत्वासे यथासुखम् ॥१३-३॥

krutam kimapi naivasyad iti sanchintya tatvatah |
yada yatkartum ayati tat krutvase yathasukham ||13-3||

In reality, I understand that no action is ever committed. Therefore, I exist happily, doing whatever presents itself to be done.

कर्मनैष्कर्म्यनिर्बन्धभावा देहस्थयोगिनः।
संयोगायोगविरहादहमासे यथासुखम् ॥१३-४॥

karma naishkarmya nirbandhabhava dehastha yoginah |
sanyoga ayoga virahad ahamase yathasukham ||13-4||

Yogis attached to their bodies are in bondage to the concepts of action and inaction. Therefore, I abandon the feelings of attachment and detachment, and exist happily in every situation.

अर्थानर्थौ न मे स्थित्या गत्या न शयनेन वा।
तिष्ठन् गच्छन् स्वपन् तस्मादहमासे यथासुखम् ॥१३-५॥

arthanartho na me sthitya gatya na shayanena va |
tishthan gachhan svapan tasmad ahamase yathasukham ||13-5||

There is no benefit or loss for me while standing or moving, sleeping, sitting, going, dreaming. Therefore, I exist happily in every situation.

स्वपतो नास्ति मे हानिः सिद्धिर्यत्नवतो न वा।
नाशोल्लासौ विहायास्मदहमासे यथासुखम् ॥१३-६॥

svapato nasti me hanih siddhiryatnavato na va |
nashot lasau vihaya asmad ahamase yathasukham ||13-6||

Sleeping causes me no harm or end of success. Therefore, abandoning lamentation and celebration, I exist happily in every situation.

सुखादिरूपा नियमं भावेष्वालोक्य भूरिशः ।
शुभाशुभे विहायास्मादहमासे यथासुखम् ॥१३-७॥

sukhadirupa niyamam bhaveshvalokya bhurishah |
shubhashubhe vihayasmad ahamase yathasukham ||13-7||

By the rules of nature, happiness etc. manifest and go out of existence endlessly. Therefore, abandoning good and bad, I exist happily in every situation.

Chapter 14

जनक उवाच -
प्रकृत्या शून्यचित्तो यः प्रमादाद् भावभावनः।
निद्रितो बोधित इव क्षीण-संस्मरणो हि सः ॥१४-१॥

janaka uvacha
prakrutya shunyachitto yah pramadad bhavabhavanah |
nidrito bodhita iva kshina samsmarano hi sah ||14-1||

Janaka said –
One whose mind is silent by nature and who does not care about existence or non-existence breaks away from past memories, like a person coming awake from a dream.

क्व धनानि क्व मित्राणि क्व मे विषयदस्यवः।
क्व शास्त्रं क्व च विज्ञानं यदा मे गलिता स्पृहा ॥१४-२॥

kva dhanani kva mitrani kva me vishayadasyavah |
kva shastram kva cha vigyanam yada me galita spruha ||14-2||

When my desires have perished, what is wealth to me, what are friends, what is sensual satisfaction, what are scriptures and what is scientific knowledge?

विज्ञाते साक्षिपुरुषे परमात्मनि चेश्वरे।
नैराश्ये बंधमोक्षे च न चिंता मुक्तये मम ॥१४-३॥

vigyate sakshipurushe paramatmani cheshvare |
nairashye bandhamokshe cha na chinta muktaye mama ||14-3||

Knowing the witness entity, who is the Supreme One, I do not worry about disappointment, bondage or liberation, and stay free!

अंतर्विकल्पशून्यस्य बहिः स्वच्छन्दचारिणः।
भ्रान्तस्येव दशास्तास्तास्-तादृशा एव जानते ॥१४-४॥

antarvikalpashunyasya bahih svachhanda charinah |
bhrantasyeva dashastastas tadrasha eva janate ||14-4||

The state that is desireless from within but is spontaneous from outside, can only be recognized by one who is in the same state.

Chapter 15

अष्टावक्र उवाच -
यथातथोपदेशेन कृतार्थः सत्त्वबुद्धिमान्।
आजीवमपि जिज्ञासुः परस्तत्र विमुह्यति ॥१५-१॥

ashtavakra uvacha
yatha tatha upadeshena krutarthah satvabuddhiman |
ajivamapi jigyasuh parastatra vimuhyati ||15-1||

Ashtavakra said –
A man with an honest mind becomes successful by following instructions exactly. Without this, even lifelong curiosity is useless.

मोक्षो विषयवैरस्यं बन्धो वैषयिको रसः।
एतावदेव विज्ञानं यथेच्छसि तथा कुरु ॥१५-२॥

moksho vishaya vairasyam bandho vaishayiko rasah |
etavad eva vigyanam yathechhasi tatha kuru ||15-2||

Indifference to senses is liberation; being interested in them is bondage. Realize this higher knowledge, then do as you like.

वाग्मिप्राज्ञामहोद्योगं जनं मूकजडालसं।
करोति तत्त्वबोधोऽयम-तस्त्यक्तो बुभुक्षभिः ॥१५-३॥

vagmi pragyam ahodyogam janam mukajadalasam |
karoti tatvabodho ayam tastyakto bubhukshabhih ||15-3||

Eloquent, wise and industrious people become mute, still and inactive after they realize the truth, so that others renounce worldly hunger too.

न त्वं देहो न ते देहो भोक्ता कर्ता न वा भवान्।
चिद्रूपोऽसि सदा साक्षी निरपेक्षः सुखं चर ॥१५-४॥

na tvam deho na te deho bhokta karta na va bhavan |
chidrupo asi sada sakshi nirapekshah sukham chara ||15-4||

Neither are you the body, nor is the body yours. Neither are you the doer of actions, nor are you the experiencer. You are consciousness, the eternal witness, one without expectations, so stay happy.

रागद्वेषौ मनोधर्मौ न मनस्ते कदाचन।
निर्विकल्पोऽसि बोधात्मा निर्विकारः सुखं चर ॥१५-५॥

ragadveshau manodharmo na manaste kadachana |
nirvikalpa asi bodhatma nirvikarah sukham chara ||15-5||

Attraction and repulsion are the nature of the mind, and you are not the mind – not at all! You are the pure conscious Self, without desires, without distortions, therefore be happy.

सर्वभूतेषु चात्मानं सर्वभूतानि चात्मनि।
विज्ञाय निरहंकारो निर्ममस्त्वं सुखी भव ॥१५-६॥

sarvabhuteshu cha atmanam sarvabhutani cha atmani |
vigyaya nirahankaro nirmamastvam sukhi bhava ||15-6||

All beings exist in the Self and the Self exists in all beings. Knowing this, be without ego, be indifferent, and be happy.

विश्वं स्फुरति यत्रेदं तरंगा इव सागरे।
तत्त्वमेव न सन्देह-श्चिन्मूर्ते विज्वरो भव ॥१५-७॥

vishvam sfurati yatredam taranga iva sagare |
tattvameva na sandehashchinmurte vijvaro bhava ||15-7||

The universe springs from you just as waves from the sea. You are consciousness itself, do not doubt that, so be without anxieties and worries.

श्रद्धस्व तात श्रद्धस्व नात्र मोऽहं कुरुष्व भोः।
ज्ञानस्वरूपो भगवानात्मा त्वं प्रकृतेः परः ॥१५-८॥

shraddhasva tata shraddhasva natra moham kurushva bhoh |
gyanasvarupo bhagavanatma tvam prakruteh parah ||15-8||

Trust yourself in this way, trust yourself! Do not be deluded. You are the Supreme Self in the form of knowledge, you are beyond nature.

गुणैः संवेष्टितो देहस्तिष्ठत्यायाति याति च।
आत्मा न गंता नागंता किमेनमनुशोचसि ॥१५-९॥

gunaih sanveshtito dehastishthatyayati yati cha |
atma na ganta naganta kimenam anushochasi ||15-9||

The body is covered with attributes of nature, and it comes, stays, and then goes. The Self neither comes nor goes, so why lament over it?

देहस्तिष्ठतु कल्पान्तं गच्छत्वद्यैव वा पुनः।
क्व वृद्धिः क्व च वा हानिस्तव चिन्मात्ररूपिणः ॥१५-१०॥

dehastishthatu kalpantam gachhat vadyaiva va punah |
kva vruddhih kva va hanistava chinmatra rupinah ||15-10||

The body may exist until the end of time, then again it may be gone. Where is the gain from it, and where is the harm? You are the state of pure consciousness!

त्वय्यनंतमहांभोधौ विश्ववीचिः स्वभावतः।
उदेतु वास्तमायातु न ते वृद्धिर्न वा क्षतिः ॥१५-११॥

tvayi anantamahambhodhau vishvavichih svabhavatah |
udetu vastam ayatu na te vruddhirna va kshatih ||15-11||

The universe rises and subsides within you naturally, as waves in an infinite ocean! But you neither gain, nor lose from it.

तात चिन्मात्ररूपोऽसि न ते भिन्नमिदं जगत्।
अतः कस्य कथं कुत्र हेयोपादेयकल्पना ॥१५-१२॥

tata chinmatra rupo asi na te bhinnam idam jagat |
atah kasya katham kurta heyopadeya Kalpana ||15-12||

You are the state of pure consciousness, and this world is not separate from you. Therefore, what can be considered unacceptable or admirable, where and how?

एकस्मिन्नव्यये शान्ते चिदाकाशेऽमले त्वयि।
कुतो जन्म कुतो कर्म कुतोऽहंकार एव च ॥१५-१३॥

ekasmin na vyaye shante chidakashe amale tvayi |
kuto janma kuto karma kuto ahankara eva cha ||15-13||

You are alone in this calm, conscious, stainless space. So where is birth, where is action, where is ego?

यत्त्वं पश्यसि तत्रैकस्त्वमेव प्रतिभाससे।
किं पृथक् भासते स्वर्णात् कटकांगदनूपुरम् ॥१५-१४॥

yattvam pashyasi tatraikastvameva pratibhasase |
kim pruthak bhasate svarnat katakangadanupuram ||15-14||

You are one, but appear as many because of your reflections. Doesn't gold appear different from bangles, armlets and anklets?

अयं सोऽहमयं नाहं विभागमिति संत्यज।
सर्वमात्मेति निश्चित्य निःसङ्कल्पः सुखी भव ॥१५-१५॥

ayam so ahamayam naham vibhagam iti santyaja |
sarvam atmeti nishchitya nih sankalpah sukhi bhava ||15-15||

That is me, and that is not me – renounce all such distinctions. Decide that your Self is everything! Have no other resolutions and be happy!

तवैवाज्ञानतो विश्वं त्वमेकः परमार्थतः।
त्वत्तोऽन्यो नास्ति संसारी नासंसारी च कश्चन ॥१५-१६॥

tavaiva agyanato vishvam tvamekah paramarthatah |
tvatto anyo nasti sansari nasansari cha kaschana ||15-16||

The universe appears real only due to ignorance. In reality, you alone exist. Apart from you, nothing exists – worldly, unworldly or otherwise!

भ्रान्तिमात्रमिदं विश्वं न किंचिदिति निश्चयी।
निर्वासनः स्फूर्तिमात्रो न किंचिदिव शाम्यति ॥१५-१७॥

bhrantimatram idam vishvam na kinchid iti nishchayi |
nirvasanah sfurtimatro na kinchid iva shamyati ||15-17||

Decide that this world is only an illusion, it is really nothing! Without annihilating desires that spring up, peace is never attained.

एक एव भवांभोधावासीदस्ति भविष्यति।
न ते बन्धोऽस्ति मोक्षो वा कृत्यकृत्यः सुखं चर ॥१५-१८॥

eka eva bhavambhodhavasidasti bhavishyati |
na te bandho asti moksho va krutya akrutyah sukham chara ||15-18||

There was, is, and will be only one ocean of existence. You are neither in bondage, nor in liberation. Exist happily, neither doing, nor non-doing.

मा सङ्कल्पविकल्पाभ्यां चित्तं क्षोभय चिन्मय।
उपशाम्य सुखं तिष्ठ स्वात्मन्यानन्दविग्रहे ॥१५-१९॥

ma sankalpa vikalpabhyam chittam kshobhaya chinmaya |
upashamya sukham tishtha sva atmani anandavigrahe ||15-19||

You are pure consciousness. Do not get agitated by various resolves of the imagination. Be at peace, be happy, and stand blissfully in your Self-state.

त्यजैव ध्यानं सर्वत्र मा किंचिद् हृदि धारय।
आत्मा त्वं मुक्त एवासि किं विमृश्य करिष्यसि ॥१५- २०॥

tyajaiva dhyanam sarvatra ma kinchid hrudi dharaya |
atma tvam mukta evasi kim vimrushya karishyasi ||15-20||

Remove your attention from everything, do not hold anything in your heart. As the Self, you are definitely free, why act with such anxiety?

Chapter 16

अष्टावक्र उवाच -
आचक्ष्व शृणु वा तात नानाशास्त्राण्यनेकशः।
तथापि न तव स्वास्थ्यं सर्वविस्मरणाद् ऋते ॥१६- १॥

ashtavakra uvacha
achakshva shrunu va tata nanashastrani anekashah |
tathapi na tava svasthyam sarva vismaranad rute ||16-1||

Ashtavakra said –
You can listen to eloquent speeches and read many varieties of scriptures, even then you will not be in an established state unless you forget everything!

भोगं कर्म समाधिं वा कुरु विज्ञ तथापि ते।
चित्तं निरस्तसर्वाशामत्यर्थं रोचयिष्यति ॥१६- २॥

bhogam karma samadhim va kuru vigya tathapi te |
chittam nirasta sarvashamatyartham rochayishyati ||16-2||

You can either experience the fruits of your actions or experience the state of Samadhi. Since you are wise, extinguishing every desire of the mind will be more pleasing to you.

आयासात्सकलो दुःखी नैनं जानाति कश्चन।
अनेनैवोपदेशेन धन्यः प्राप्नोति निर्वृतिम् ॥१६- ३॥

ayasat sakalo dukhi nainam janati kashchana |
anenaiva upadeshena dhanyah prapnoti nirvrutim ||16-3||

It is because of effort that everyone is unhappy, but nobody knows that. It is with this superior teaching that the blessed ones attain liberation.

व्यापारे खिद्यते यस्तु निमेषोन्मेषयोरपि।
तस्यालस्य धुरीणस्य सुखं नन्यस्य कस्यचित् ॥१६-४॥

vyapare khidyate yastu nimeshon meshayorapi |
tasyalasya dhurinasya sukham nanyasya kasyachit ||16-4||

Happiness belongs only to the greatly lazy person who considers even blinking his eyelashes a wearisome exertion, and nobody else!

इदं कृतमिदं नेति द्वंद्वैर्मुक्तं यदा मनः।
धर्मार्थकाममोक्षेषु निरपेक्षं तदा भवेत् ॥१६-५॥

idam krutam idam neti dvandvairmuktam yada manah |
dharmartha kama moksheshu nirapeksham tada bhavet ||16-5||

When the mind is free from dualities like "This is to be done, and not that", then it truly becomes indifferent to righteousness, wealth, lust and liberation.

विरक्तो विषयद्वेष्टा रागी विषयलोलुपः।
ग्रहमोक्षविहीनस्तु न विरक्तो न रागवान् ॥१६-६॥

virakto vishayadveshta ragi vishayalolupah |
grahamoksha vihinastu na virakto na ragavan ||16-6||

The passionless one is averse to the senses; the passionate one is excessively fond of the senses. But you are without the desire to either grasp or be liberated, you are neither passionless nor passionate.

हेयोपादेयता तावत्संसारविटपांकुरः।
स्पृहा जीवति यावद् वै निर्विचारदशास्पदम् ॥१६-७॥

heyopadeyata tavat sansaravitapankurah |
spruha jivato yavad vai nirvicharad ashaspadam ||16-7||

As long as there is craving for life, as long as there is a sense of falling down or being exalted, the seed of the tree of this world still exists. Therefore, stand still in the state of no-thought.

प्रवृत्तौ जायते रागो निर्वृत्तौ द्वेष एव हि।
निर्द्वन्द्वो बालवद् धीमान् एवमेव व्यवस्थितः ॥१६-८॥

pravruttau jayate rago nivruttau dvesha eva hi |
nirdvandvo balavad dhiman evam eva vyavasthitah ||16-8||

Action gives birth to attachment; lack of action gives birth to aversion. The wise should be child-like, indifferent to such dualities, and stay established like that.

हातुमिच्छति संसारं रागी दुःखजिहासया।
वीतरागो हि निर्दुःखस्-तस्मिन्नपि न खिद्यति ॥१६-९॥

hatum ichhati sansaram ragi dukhajihasaya |
vitarago hi nirdukhas tasmin na api na khidyati ||16-9||

One attached to senses desires to give up the world in order to get rid of his sorrows. However, it is only through non-attachment that one can be without sorrows, and never get disturbed.

यस्याभिमानो मोक्षेऽपि देहेऽपि ममता तथा।
न च ज्ञानी न वा योगी केवलं दुःखभागसौ ॥१६-१०॥

yasya abhimano moksha api dehe api mamata tatha |
na cha gyani na va yogi kevalam dukhabhagasau ||16-10||

The one who takes pride in liberation, yet maintains an affinity towards the body, is neither wise, nor a yogi. He is just a sufferer.

हरो यद्युपदेष्टा ते हरिः कमलजोऽपि वा।
तथापि न तव स्वाथ्यं सर्वविस्मरणाद्दते ॥१६-११॥

haro yadyupadeshta harih kamalajo api va |
tathapi na tava svathyam sarva vismaranadrate ||16-11||

Shiva, Vishnu and Brahma themselves may instruct you, yet you will not be in an established state unless you forget everything!

Chapter 17

अष्टावक्र उवाच
तेन ज्ञानफलं प्राप्तं योगाभ्यासफलं तथा।
तृप्तः स्वच्छेन्द्रियो नित्यं एकाकी रमते तु यः ॥१७-१॥

ashtavakra uvacha
tena gyanaphalam praptam yogabhyasa phalam tatha |
truptah svachhendriyo nityam ekaki ramate tu yah ||17-1||

Ashtavakra said –
The fruits of wisdom and the fruits of the study of yoga both belong to him who is content, who is always of purified senses, and who enjoys solitude.

न कदाचिज्जगत्यस्मिन् तत्त्वज्ञा हन्त खिद्यति।
यत एकेन तेनेदं पूर्णं ब्रह्माण्डमण्डलम् ॥१७-२॥

na kadachit jagati asmin tattvagya hanta khidyati |
yata ekena tenedam purnam brahmanda mandalam ||17-2||

The one who knows the truth is not disturbed by any trouble of any kind in this world. For he himself alone comprises this entire cosmos!

न जातु विषयाः केऽपि स्वारामं हर्षयन्त्यमी।
सल्लकीपल्लवप्रीतमिवेभं निंबपल्लवाः ॥१७-३॥

na jatu vishayah kea pi svaramam harshayantyami |
sallaki pallava pritam ivebham nimbapallavah ||17-3||

65

None of the senses can bring joy to the one who rests in himself – it is like offering neem leaves to the elephant that likes Sallaki leaves.

यस्तु भोगेषु भुक्तेषु न भवत्यधिवासिता।
अभुक्तेषु निराकांक्षी तदृशो भवदुर्लभः ॥१७-४॥

yastu bhogeshu bhukteshu na bhavatya adhivasita |
abhukteshu nirakankshi tadrasho bhavadurlabhah ||17-4||

It is rare to find a person who neither dwells on pleasures enjoyed in the past, nor longs for pleasures not yet experienced!

बुभुक्षुरिह संसारे मुमुक्षुरपि दृश्यते।
भोगमोक्षनिराकांक्षी विरलो हि महाशयः ॥१७-५॥

bubhukshuriha sansare mumukshurapi drashyate |
bhogamoksha nirakankshi viralo hi mahashayah ||17-5||

In this world, there are those who hunger for worldly pleasures, and those who hunger for liberation. But rare is that great man who is desireless of either worldly pleasures or liberation!

धर्मार्थकाममोक्षेषु जीविते मरणे तथा।
कस्याप्युदारचित्तस्य हेयोपादेयता न हि ॥१७-६॥

dharma artha kama moksheshu jivite marane tatha |
kasyapi udarachittasya heyopadeyata na hi ||17-6||

Where is that lofty soul who feels neither rejection nor attraction to righteousness, wealth, lust, liberation, life or death!

वांछा न विश्वविलये न द्वेषस्तस्य च स्थितौ।
यथा जीविकया तस्माद् धन्य आस्ते यथा सुखम् ॥१७-७॥

vanchha na vishvavilaye na dveshastasya cha sthitau |
yatha jivikaya tasmad dhania aste yatha sukham ||17-7||

He neither desires the end of this world, nor despises its continued existence. He lives life as it is, always blessed, always happy.

कृतार्थोऽनेन ज्ञानेनेत्येवं गलितधीः कृती।
पश्यन् शृण्वन् स्पृशन् जिघ्रन्न् अश्नन्नस्ते यथा सुखम् ॥१७-८॥

krutartha anena gyanena eti evam galitadhih kruti |
pashyan shrunvan sprushan jighrann ashnan naste yatha sukham ||17-8||

Having achieved this widom which melts the external persona, he remains happy while seeing, hearing, touching, smelling, eating (using the senses).

शून्या दृष्टिर्वृथा चेष्टा विकलानीन्द्रियाणि च।
न स्पृहा न विरक्तिर्वा क्षीणसंसारसागरे ॥१७-९॥

shunya drashtivrutha cheshta vikalani indriyani cha |
na spruha na viraktirva kshina samsara sagare ||17-9||

His focus empty, desires discarded, senses disempowered, he neither longs for, nor rejects this miserable ocean of existence.

न जगर्ति न निद्राति नोन्मीलति न मीलति।
अहो परदशा क्वापि वर्तते मुक्तचेतसः ॥१७-१०॥

na jagarti na nidrati nonmilati na milati |
aho paradasha kvapi vartate muktachetasah ||17-10||

Indeed, rare is the one with such liberated consciousness who stays in the state where there is no waking, no sleeping, no opening, nor closing of the eyes!

सर्वत्र दृश्यते स्वस्थः सर्वत्र विमलाशयः।
समस्तवासना मुक्तो मुक्तः सर्वत्र राजते ॥१७-११॥

sarvatra drashyate svasthah sarvatra vimalashayah |
samasta vasana mukto muktah sarvatra rajate ||17-11||

That truly liberated one shines everywhere, who sees everything as one whole, who has beneficial intentions towards everything, who is free from every form of lust.

पश्यन् शृण्वन् स्पृशन् जिघ्रन्न् अश्नन् गृण्हन् वदन् व्रजन्।
ईहितानीहितैर्मुक्तो मुक्त एव महाशयः ॥१७-१२॥

pashyan shrunvan sprushan jighrann ashnan grunhan vadan vrajan |
ihitani hitaih mukto mukta eva mahashayah ||17-12||

Desireless in seeing, hearing, touching, smelling, eating, consuming, talking, walking, even in desiring, such a great person is truly liberated!

न निन्दति न च स्तौति न हृष्यति न कुप्यति।
न ददाति न गृण्हाति मुक्तः सर्वत्र नीरसः ॥१७-१३॥

na nindati na cha stauti na hrushyati na kupyati |
na dadati na grunhati muktah sarvatra nirasah ||17-13||

He neither blames nor praises, is neither thrilled nor angry, neither gives nor takes. He is indifferent to everything and is truly free!

सानुरागां स्त्रियं दृष्ट्वा मृत्युं वा समुपस्थितं।
अविह्वलमनाः स्वस्थो मुक्त एव महाशयः ॥१७-१४॥

sanuragam striyam drashtva mrutyum va samupasthitam |
avihavalamanah svastho mukta eva mahashayah ||17-14||

One who remains steady, and in whom no feeling arises when faced with either impassioned women, or death – such a great man is truly liberated!

सुखे दुःखे नरे नार्यां संपत्सु विपत्सु च।
विशेषो नैव धीरस्य सर्वत्र समदर्शिनः ॥१७-१५॥

sukhe dukhe nare naryam sampatsu vipatsu cha |
vishesho naiva dhirasya sarvatra samadarshinah ||17-15||

For the wise, there is no difference between happiness and sorrow, men and women, fortune and misfortune – he sees these all alike.

न हिंसा नैव कारुण्यं नौद्धत्यं न च दीनता।
नाश्चर्यं नैव च क्षोभः क्षीणसंसरणे नरे ॥१७-१६॥

na hinsa naiva karunyam nauddhatyam na cha dinata |
nashcharyam naiva cha kshobhah kshinasansarane nare ||17-16||

There is neither violence nor compassion, neither pride nor poverty, neither astonishment nor disturbance in the man who is unattached to this feeble existence.

न मुक्तो विषयद्वेष्टा न वा विषयलोलुपः।
असंसक्तमना नित्यं प्राप्ताप्राप्तमुपाश्नुते ॥१७-१७॥

na mukto vishayadveshta na va vishayalolupah |
asansaktamana nityam praptapraptam upashnute ||17-17||

The liberated one is neither repulsed by obects of the senses, nor attracted to them. He is always of unattached mind, whether faced with achievement or non-achievement.

समाधानसमाधान-हिताहितविकल्पनाः।
शून्यचित्तो न जानाति कैवल्यमिव संस्थितः ॥१७-१८॥

samadhan asamadhana hitahita vikalpanah |
shunyachitto na janati kaivalyam iva sansthitah ||17-18||

The one with a blank consciousness does not know problems or solutions, good or bad, and has no fantasies. He merely remains established in the Self.

निर्ममो निरहंकारो न किंचिदिति निश्चितः ।
अन्तर्गलितसर्वाशः कुर्वन्नपि करोति न ॥१७-१९॥

nirmamo nirahankaro na kinchit iti nishchitah |
antargalita sarvashah kurvannapi karoti na ||17-19||

He is indifferent, non-egotistic, has no fixed ideas about anything. He for whom everything has dissolved in oneself, does nothing even when he acts.

मनःप्रकाशसंमोहस्वप्नजाड्यविवर्जितः ।
दशां कामपि संप्राप्तो भवेद् गलितमानसः ॥१७-२०॥

manah prakasha sanmoha svapnajadya vivarjitah |
dasham kamapi samprapto bhaved galitamanasah ||17-20||

His mind is illuminated and free of delusions, dreams and desires, who has attained a state of being completely dissolved in the Self.

Chapter 18

अष्टावक्र उवाच
यस्य बोधोदये तावत्स्वप्नवद् भवति भ्रमः।
तस्मै सुखैकरूपाय नमः शान्ताय तेजसे ॥१८-१॥

ashtavakra uvacha
yasya bodhodaye tavatsvapnavad bhavati bhramah |
tasmai sukhaika rupaya namah shantaya tejase ||18-1||

Ashtavakra said –
I bow to that singular, serene, blissful light of consciousness, on the awakening of which, delusions are understood to be insubstantial like dreams.

अर्जयित्वाखिलान् अर्थान् भोगानाप्नोति पुष्कलान्।
न हि सर्वपरित्याजमन्तरेण सुखी भवेत् ॥१८-२॥

arjayitvakhilan arthan bhogan apnoti pushkalan |
na hi sarvaparityajamantarena sukhi bhavet ||18-2||

By accumulating a lot of wealth, one may obtain great pleasure. However, one cannot be happy without its internal renunciation.

कर्तव्यदुःखमार्तण्डज्वाला दग्धान्तरात्मनः।
कुतः प्रशमपीयूषधारासारमृते सुखम् ॥१८-३॥

kartavya dukham artanda jvala dagdha antaratmanah |
kutah prashamapiyushadharasara amrute sukham ||18-3||

When the blaze of duty, sorrow, blame burns the inner self, where is the calm nectar-stream of bliss?

भवोऽयं भावनामात्रो न किंचित् परमर्थतः।
नास्त्यभावः स्वभावनां भावाभावविभाविनाम् ॥१८-४॥

bhavo ayam bhavan amatro na kinchit paramarthatah |
nasti abhavah svabhavanam bhava abhava vibhavinam ||18-4||

This existence is merely imagination, it is nothing in reality. The one who understands that existence and non-existence occur naturally, spontaneously, never ceases to exist!

न दूरं न च संकोचाल्लब्धमेवात्मनः पदं।
निर्विकल्पं निरायासंनिर्विकारं निरंजनम् ॥१८-५॥

na duram na cha sankochat labdham evatmanah padam |
nirvikalpam nirayasannirvikaram niranjanam ||18-5||

Neither is this state of the Self far away, nor can it be achieved by hesitation. It is beyond imagination, effortless, unchangeable, stainless.

व्यामोहमात्रविरतौ स्वरूपादानमात्रतः।
वीतशोका विराजन्ते निरावरणदृष्टयः ॥१८-६॥

vyamoham atra viratau svarupadan amatratah |
vitashoko virajante niravarana drashtayah ||18-6||

One's bewilderment ceases just by renouncing external form. Then one's vision becomes sorrowless, brilliant, unclouded!

समस्तं कल्पनामात्रमात्मा मुक्तः सनातनः ।
इति विज्ञाय धीरो हि किमभ्यस्यति बालवत् ॥१८-७॥

samastam kalpanamatram atma muktah sanatanah |
iti vigyaya dhiro hi kimabhyasyati balavat ||18-7||

Everything is just imagination, the self is eternally free. Knowing this, how can the wise one behave so childishly?

आत्मा ब्रह्मेति निश्चित्य भावाभावौ च कल्पितौ ।
निष्कामः किं विजानाति किं ब्रूते च करोति किम् ॥१८-८॥

atma brahmeti nishchitya bhavabhavau cha kalpitau |
nishkamah kim vijanati kim brute cha karoti kim ||18-8||

Knowing decisively that the Self is the Absolute, and being and non-being are imagined, what is there for the one without desires to learn, speak, or do?

अयं सोऽहमयं नाहं इति क्षीणा विकल्पना ।
सर्वमात्मेति निश्चित्य तूष्णींभूतस्य योगिनः ॥१८-९॥

ayam so aham ayam naham iti kshina vikalpana |
sarvam atmeti nishchitya turshnibhutasya yoginah ||18-9||

"I am this" and "I am not this" these are all worn away in a yogi who has decided firmly that "I am everything there is", and whose longings have become a thing of the past.

न विक्षेपो न चैकाग्र्यं नातिबोधो न मूढता।
न सुखं न च वा दुःखं उपशान्तस्य योगिनः ॥१८-१०॥

na vikshepo na chaikakyam natibodho na mudhata |
na sukham na cha va dukham upashantasya yoginah ||18-10||

There is neither distraction nor concentration, neither higher knowledge nor ignorance, neither happiness nor sorrow for the completely tranquil yogi.

स्वाराज्ये भैक्षवृत्तौ चलाभालाभे जने वने।
निर्विकल्पस्वभावस्यन विशेषोऽस्ति योगिनः ॥१८-११॥

svarajye bhaikshavruttau chalabhalabhe jane vane |
nirvikalpasvabhavasyan vishesho asti yoginah ||18-11||

The kingdom of heaven or the profession of begging, gain or loss, life among people or in the forest, are all indistinct to the yogi whose nature is unwavering.

क्व धर्मः क्व च वा कामः क्व चार्थः क्व विवेकिता।
इदं कृतमिदं नेति द्वन्द्वैर्मुक्तस्य योगिनः ॥१८-१२॥

kva dharmah kva cha va kamah kva cha arthah kva vivekita |
idam krutam idam neti dvandvaih muktasya yoginah ||18-12||

What is righteousness, what is lust, what is wealth and what is discrimination for the yogi who is free from dualities like "I have done this" and "I have not done this".

कृत्यं किमपि नैवास्तिन कापि हृदि रंजना।
यथा जीवनमेवेह जीवन्मुक्तस्य योगिनः ॥१८-१३॥

krutyam kimapi naivastina kapi hridi ranjana |
yatha jivanam eveha jivanmuktasya yoginah ||18-13||

There is nothing that needs to be done, nor any delight to his heart. Thus, even while deeply alive, the yogi is free from life!

क्व मोहः क्व च वा विश्वं क्व तद् ध्यानं क्व मुक्तता।
सर्वसंकल्पसीमायां विश्रान्तस्य महात्मनः ॥१८-१४॥

kva mohah kva cha va vishvam kva tad dhyanam kva muktata |
sarvasankalpa simayam vishrantasya mahatmanah ||18-14||

Where is attachment, where is the universe, where is meditation or liberation? Having understood the end limit of all endeavours, the great soul rests!

येन विश्वमिदं दृष्टं स नास्तीति करोतु वै।
निर्वासनः किं कुरुते पश्यन्नपि न पश्यति ॥१८-१५॥

yena vishvam idam drashtam sa nasti iti karotu vai |
nirvasanah kim kurute pashyann api na pashyati ||18-15||

The one who sees this universe may come to understand that it does not exist. But how can the desireless one do this? Even in seeing, he does not see!

येन दृष्टं परं ब्रह्म सोऽहं ब्रह्मेति चिन्तयेत्।
किं चिन्तयति निश्चिन्तो यो न पश्यति ॥१८-१६॥

yena drashtam param brahma soham brahmeti chintayet |
kim chintayati nishchinto yo na pashyati ||18-16||

He who sees the Supreme Absolute may come to contemplate "I am that Absolute". But what can he contemplate, who is without thought, and who does not see!

दृष्टो येनात्मविक्षेपो निरोधं कुरुते त्वसौ।
उदारस्तु न विक्षिप्तः साध्याभावात्करोति किम् ॥१८-१७॥

drashto yena atmavikshepo nirodham kurute dvasau |
udarastu na vikshiptah sadhyabhavat karoti kim ||18-17||

He who sees distraction in himself may accomplish correcting it. But not so the noble, non-distracted one – what is there for him to accomplish!

धीरो लोकविपर्यस्तो वर्तमानोऽपि लोकवत्।
नो समाधिं न विक्षेपं न लोपं स्वस्य पश्यति ॥१८-१८॥

dhiro lokaviparyasto vartamana api lokavat |
no samadhim na vikshepam na lopam svasya pashyati ||18-18||

The wise one, contrary to worldly people, even while living presently amongst them, perceives no meditative state, no distraction, no deficiency in oneself.

भावाभावविहीनो यस्तृप्तो निर्वासनो बुधः ।
नैव किंचित्कृतं तेनलोकदृष्ट्या विकुर्वता ॥१८-१९॥

bhavabhavavihino yastrupto nirvasano budhah |
naiva kinchit krutam tena lokadrashtya vikurvata ||18-19||

The wise one who is above the states of being and non-being, who is desireless and content, is not the doer of any action, even if he does act in the eyes of the people.

प्रवृत्तौ वा निवृत्तौ वा नैव धीरस्य दुर्ग्रहः ।
यदा यत्कर्तुमायातितत्कृत्वा तिष्ठते सुखम् ॥१८-२०॥

pravruttau va nivruttau va naiva dhirasya durgrahah |
yada yatkartum ayati tat krutva tishthate sukham ||18-20||

Whether doing something or doing nothing, the wise is never inconvenienced. He does whatever presents itself to be done, and he stays happy.

निर्वासनो निरालंबः स्वच्छन्दो मुक्तबन्धनः ।
क्षिप्तः संस्कारवातेन चेष्टते शुष्कपर्णवत् ॥१८-२१॥

nirvasano niralambah svachhando muktabandhanah |
kshiptah sanskaravatena cheshtate shushka parnavat ||18-21||

Who is desireless, independent, following his own will, free from all bonds is like a withered leaf scattered around by the wind of sanskaras.

असंसारस्य तु क्वापि न हर्षो न विषादिता।
स शीतलहमना नित्यं विदेह इव राजये ॥१८- २२॥

asansarasya tu kvapi na harsho na vishadita |
sa shitalahamana nityam videha iva rajaye ||18-22||

The one who is beyond samsara (the world) has no joy and no lamentation. He is kingly, always with a serene mind, as if without a body.

कुत्रापि न जिहासास्ति नाशो वापि न कुत्रचित्।
आत्मारामस्य धीरस्य शीतलाच्छतरात्मनः ॥१८- २३॥

kutrapi na jihasasti nasho vapi na kutrachit |
atmaramasya dhirasya shitalat shataratmanah ||18-23||

Where is the sense of renouncing anything, or feeling a sense of loss in anything for the wise one whose inner desires have calmed, who rests only in himself!

प्रकृत्या शून्यचित्तस्य कुर्वतोऽस्य यदृच्छया।
प्राकृतस्येव धीरस्य न मानो नावमानता ॥१८- २४॥

prakrutya shunya chittasya kurvata asya yadrat shaya |
prakrutasyeva dhirasya na mano navamanata ||18-24||

For a man who is wise by nature, who naturally holds silence in his heart and does as he pleases, there is neither honour nor disgrace.

कृतं देहेन कर्मेदं न मया शुद्धरूपिणा।
इति चिन्तानुरोधी यः कुर्वन्नपि करोति न ॥१८- २५॥

krutam dehena karmedam na maya shuddha rupina |
iti chinta anurodhi yah kurvan api karoti na ||18-25||

"This action is done by the body, not by me who is pure of form" – the one who respects this thinking does nothing, even when he acts.

अतद्वादीव कुरुते न भवेदपि बालिशः।
जीवन्मुक्तः सुखी श्रीमान् संसरन्नपि शोभते ॥१८- २६॥

atadvadiva kurute na bhavedapi balishah |
jivanmuktah sukhi shriman sansarannapi shobhate ||18-26||

The one who acts (spontaneously) without saying why is not immature. He is free from the bondage of life even while he lives. He is happy, blessed, and shines splendidly, even within samsara!

नाविचारसुश्रान्तो धीरो विश्रान्तिमागतः।
न कल्पते न जाति न शृणोति न पश्यति ॥१८- २७॥

navicharasushranto dhiro vishrantim agatah |
na kalpate na jati na shrunoti na pashyati ||18-27||

The wise one who has reached the end of all thoughts and finally rests in himself, does not imagine, does not know, does not hear or see.

असमाधेरविक्षेपान् न मुमुक्षुर्न चेतरः।
निश्चित्य कल्पितं पश्यन् ब्रह्मैवास्ते महाशयः ॥१८- २८॥

asamadhera vikshepan na mumukshuh na chetarah |
nishchitya kalpitam pashyan brahmaiva aste mahashayah ||18-28||

The great one who is beyond the meditative state or distraction, who is not desirous of liberation or anything else, who decides that everything that is seen is imagined, becomes the very Absolute!

यस्यान्तः स्यादहंकारो न करोति सः।
निरहंकारधीरेण न किंचिदकृतं कृतम् ॥१८- २९॥

yasyantah syad ahankaro na karoti sah |
nirahankara dhirena na kinchit akrutam krutam ||18-29||

If one has ego within, he becomes a doer even when not doing anything. But the wise one who is without ego does nothing, even when he does.

नोद्विग्नं न च सन्तुष्टमकर्तृ स्पन्दवर्जितम्।
निराशं गतसन्देहं चित्तं मुक्तस्य राजते ॥१८- ३०॥

nodvignam na cha santushtam akartru spandavarjitam |
nirasham gatasandeham chittam muktasya rajate ||18-30||

The one with a liberated mind is neither disturbed nor delighted, he is unwavering, he is without desires, without doubt – he stays like a king!

निर्ध्यातुं चेष्टितुं वापि यच्चित्तं न प्रवर्तते।
निर्निमित्तमिदं किंतु निर्ध्यायेति विचेष्टते ॥१८- ३१॥

nirdhyatum cheshtitum vapi yat chittam na pravartate |
nirnimittam idam kitum nirdhyayeti vicheshtate ||18-31||

The one whose consciousness is awakened does not set off to meditate or exert himself. However, the one who does not yet know the correct direction, keeps on contemplating and exerting oneself.

तत्त्वं यथार्थमाकर्ण्य मन्दः प्राप्नोति मूढतां।
अथवा याति संकोचममूढः कोऽपि मूढवत् ॥१८-३२॥

tattvam yathartham akarnya mandah prapnoti mudhatam |
athava yati sankocham amudhah ka api mudhavat ||18-32||

The foolish man is bewildered when he hears the absolute truth. Even the clever man proceeds hesitatingly just like the fool.

एकाग्रता निरोधो वा मूढैरभ्यस्यते भृशं।
धीराः कृत्यं न पश्यन्ति सुप्तवत्स्वपदे स्थिताः ॥१८-३३॥

ekagrata nirodha va mudhairabhyasyate bhrusham |
dhirah krutyam na pashyanti suptavat svapade sthitah ||18-33||

The foolish practice concentration and non-distraction quite vehemently. The wise do not see anything more to be done, and stay within themselves as if asleep.

अप्रयत्नात् प्रयत्नाद् वा मूढो नाप्नोति निर्वृतिं।
तत्त्वनिश्चयमात्रेण प्राज्ञो भवति निर्वृतः ॥१८-३४॥

aprayatnat prayatnad va mudho na apnoti nirvrutim |
tattva nishchaya matrena pragyo bhavati nirvrutah ||18-34||

The fool does not attain liberation by trying or giving up trying. But the wise one attains liberation simply by deciding to know the truth!

शुद्धं बुद्धं प्रियं पूर्णं निष्प्रपंचं निरामयं।
आत्मानं तं न जानन्ति तत्राभ्यासपरा जनाः ॥१८- ३५॥

shuddham buddham priyam purnam nishprapancham niramayam |
atmanam tam na jananti tatra abhyasapara janah ||18-35||

Even with various practices, people do not realize the Self as pure, aware, beautiful, complete, beyond deceit, unblemished.

नाप्नोति कर्मणा मोक्षं विमूढोऽभ्यासरूपिणा।
धन्यो विज्ञानमात्रेण मुक्तस्तिष्ठत्यविक्रियः ॥१८- ३६॥

na apnoti karmana moksham vimudho abhyasa rupina |
dhanyo vigyanamatrena muktastishthati vikriyah ||18-36||

The foolish do not achieve liberation even through various practices, but the blessed ones stay free and actionless simply by knowing the higher truth.

मूढो नाप्नोति तद् ब्रह्म यतो भवितुमिच्छति।
अनिच्छन्नपि धीरो हि परब्रह्मस्वरूपभाक् ॥१८- ३७॥

mudho napnoti tad brahma yato bhavitum ichhati |
anichhan api dhiro hi parabrahma svarupabhak ||18-37||

The foolish do not achieve the Absolute even though they want it desperately, while the wise ones achieve the state of the Absolute even without wanting it.

निराधारा ग्रहव्यग्रा मूढाः संसारपोषकाः।
एतस्यानर्थमूलस्य मूलच्छेदः कृतो बुधैः ॥१८- ३८॥

niradhara grahavyagra mudhah sansara poshakah |
etasyan arthamulasya mulat shedah kruto budhaih ||18-38||

The foolish ones nourish samsara (the world) in their unchecked eagerness to grasp everything, while the wise have destroyed the very root of such evil.

न शान्तिं लभते मूढो यतः शमितुमिच्छति।
धीरस्तत्त्वं विनिश्चित्य सर्वदा शान्तमानसः ॥१८- ३९॥

na shantim labhate mudho yatah shamitum ichhati |
dhirastattvam vinishchitya sarvada shantamanasah ||18-39||

The foolish ones do not obtain peace even when they desire cessation, while the wise ones are truly always peaceful minded without even determining to do so!

क्वात्मनो दर्शनं तस्य यद् दृष्टमवलंबते।
धीरास्तं तं न पश्यन्ति पश्यन्त्यात्मानमव्ययम् ॥१८- ४०॥

kvatmano darshanam tasya yad drashtam avalambate |
dhirastam tam na pashyanti pashyanti atmanam avyayam ||18-40||

Where is the glimpse of the real Self for the one who is dependent upon what he sees? The wise one does not see all this, he only sees the Self as unchanging, imperishable!

क्व निरोधो विमूढस्य यो निर्बन्धं करोति वै ।
स्वारामस्यैव धीरस्य सर्वदासावकृत्रिमः ॥१८-४१॥

kva nirodho vimudhasya yo nirbandham karoti vai |
svaram asyaiva dhirasya sarvad asava krutrimah ||18-41||

Where is cessation for the fool who strives for it! Yet for the wise one who rests in himself always, it comes effortlessly.

भावस्य भावकः कश्चिन् न किंचिद् भावकोपरः ।
उभयाभावकः कश्चिद् एवमेव निराकुलः ॥१८-४२॥

bhavasya bhavakah kaschin na kinchid bhavakoparah |
ubhaya bhavakah kaschid evameva nirakulah ||18-42||

Some sentimentalists believe in a supreme being, some people immune to sentiment believe there is no such thing. Some are beyond both views, and therefore free from disturbance.

शुद्धमद्वयमात्मानं भावयन्ति कुबुद्धयः ।
न तु जानन्ति संमोहाद्यावज्जीवमनिर्वृताः ॥१८-४३॥

shuddham advayam atmanam bhavayanti kubuddhayah |
na tu jananti sanmohad yavat jivam anirvrutah ||18-43||

Foolish ones may believe the Self is pure and non-dual. But being mired in illusion, they do not actually know the Self, and hence they remain unfulfilled all their lives.

मुमुक्षोर्बुद्धिरालंबमन्तरेण न विद्यते।
निरालंबैव निष्कामा बुद्धिर्मुक्तस्य सर्वदा ॥१८- ४४॥

mumukshorbuddhih alambam antarena na vidyate |
niralambaiva nishkama buddhih muktasya sarvada ||18-44||

The mind that seeks liberation knows no refuge within, whereas the liberated mind remains desireless even without a refuge.

विषयद्वीपिनो वीक्ष्य चकिताः शरणार्थिनः।
विशन्ति झटिति क्रोडं निरोधैकाग्रसिद्धये ॥१८- ४५॥

vishayad vipino vikshya chakitah sharanarthinah |
vishanti jhatiti krodam nirodha ekagra siddhaye ||18-45||

The wondrous tigers of the senses frighten refuge-seekers, who immediately enter a cave in search of cessation of thought and concentration.

निर्वासनं हरिं दृष्ट्वा तूष्णीं विषयदन्तिनः।
पलायन्ते न शक्तास्ते सेवन्ते कृतचाटवः ॥१८- ४६॥

nirvasanam harim drashtva tushnim vishayad antinah |
palayante na shaktaste sevante krutachatavah ||18-46||

But seeing the desireless lion, the greedy elephants of the senses flee, and if they cannot, they become cowering servants.

न मुक्तिकारिकां धत्ते निःशङ्को युक्तमानसः।
पश्यन् शृण्वन् स्पृशन् जिघ्रन्नश्नन्नास्ते यथासुखम् ॥१८-४७॥

na mukti karikam dhatte nihshanko yuktamanasah |
pashyan shrunvan sprushan jighrann ashnan na aste yathasukham ||18-47||

The one of established mind who is without doubts and free of torment stays happy whether in seeing, hearing, touching, smelling or eating.

वस्तुश्रवणमात्रेण शुद्धबुद्धिर्निराकुलः।
नैवाचारमनाचारमौदास्यं वा प्रपश्यति ॥१८-४८॥

vastushravana matrena shuddha buddhih nirakulah |
naiva acharam anachara maudasyam va prapashyati ||18-48||

The one of pure mind becomes calm and steady on just hearing the truth. He does not see cause to do anything nor to avoid anything, nor to be indifferent.

यदा यत्कर्तुमायाति तदा तत्कुरुते ऋजुः।
शुभं वाप्यशुभं वापि तस्य चेष्टा हि बालवत् ॥१८-४९॥

yada yatkartum ayati tada tat kurute rujuh |
shubham vapyashubham vapi tasya cheshta hi balavat ||18-49||

The benevolent one does whatever presents itself to be done, good or bad. His actions are child-like.

स्वातंत्र्यात्सुखमाप्नोति स्वातंत्र्याल्लभते परं।
स्वातंत्र्यान्निर्वृतिं गच्छेत्स्वातंत्र्यात् परमं पदम् ॥१८-५०॥

svatantryat sukham apnoti svatantryat labhate param |
svatantryat nivruttim gachhet svatantryat paramam padam ||18-50||

By (inner) freedom is happiness attained, by inner freedom is the Supreme attained. By freedom is liberation attained, by freedom is the Supreme state attained!

अकर्तृत्वमभोक्तृत्वं स्वात्मनो मन्यते यदा।
तदा क्षीणा भवन्त्येव समस्ताश्चित्तवृत्तयः ॥१८-५१॥

akartrutvam abhoktrutvam svatmano manyate yada |
tada kshina bhavanti ena samasta ashchitta avruttayah ||18-51||

When one believes oneself is neither the doer nor the experiencer, then all the inconsequential waves of the mind that still exist come to an end.

उच्छृंखलाप्यकृतिका स्थितिर्धीरस्य राजते।
न तु सस्पृहचित्तस्य शान्तिर्मूढस्य कृत्रिमा ॥१८-५२॥

utshrunkhalapi akrutika sthitih dhirasya rajate |
na tu saspruhat chittasya shantih mudhasya krutrima ||18-52||

Even the irrational or silly behaviour of the wise one is resplendent, while even the deliberate calmness of the fool is artificial.

विलसन्ति महाभोगैर्विशन्ति गिरिगह्वरान्।
निरस्तकल्पना धीरा अबद्धा मुक्तबुद्धयः ॥१८-५३॥

vilasanti mahabhogaih vishanti girigahavaran |
nirastakalpana dhira abaddha mukta buddhayah ||18-53||

The wise ones who have discarded fancifulness, who are unbounded, and with liberated consciousness may enjoy themselves amidst a great number of possessions or go off to a cave in the mountains.

श्रोत्रियं देवतां तीर्थमङ्गनां भूपतिं प्रियं।
दृष्ट्वा संपूज्य धीरस्य न कापि हृदि वासना ॥१८-५४॥

shrotriyam devatam tirtham anganam bhupatim priyam |
drashtva sanpujya dhirasya na kapi hrudi vasana ||18-54||

There is no desire in the heart of a venerable wise man whether he sees a Brahmin, a celestial being, a holy place, a woman, a king or a friend.

भृत्यैः पुत्रैः कलत्रैश्च दौहित्रैश्चापि गोत्रजैः।
विहस्य धिक्कृतो योगी न याति विकृतिं मनाक् ॥१८-५५॥

bhrutyaih putraih kalatraih cha dauhitraishcha api gotrajaih |
vihasya dhikkruto yogi na yati vikrutim manak ||18-55||

In a yogi, there is not the slightest deviation whether he is laughed at or derided by servants, sons, wives, grandchildren or other relatives.

सन्तुष्टोऽपि न सन्तुष्टः खिन्नोऽपि न च खिद्यते।
तस्याश्चर्यदशां तां तादृशा एव जानते ॥१८-५६॥

santushto api na santushtah khinna api na cha khidyate |
tasyascharyadasham tam tadrasha eva janate ||18-56||

Even when content, he is not content. Even when distressed, he is not disturbed. Only those in the same state as him can know the astonishing state of such a man!

कर्तव्यतैव संसारो न तां पश्यन्ति सूरयः।
शून्याकारा निराकारा निर्विकारा निरामयाः ॥१८-५७॥

kartavyataiva sansaro na tam pashyanti surayah |
shunyakara nirakara nirvikara niramayah ||18-57||

It is the sense of duty that is worldly existence (samsara). The wise ones do not perceive it. Their state is empty, formless, changeless and untainted.

अकुर्वन्नपि संक्षोभाद् व्यग्रः सर्वत्र मूढधीः।
कुर्वन्नपि तु कृत्यानि कुशलो हि निराकुलः ॥१८-५८॥

akurvan api sankshobhat vyagrah sarvatra mudhadhih |
kurvan api tu krutyani kushalo hi nirakulah ||18-58||

Even while doing nothing, the fool is always riotous and agitated. While the skilled one is unagitated even when doing what needs to be done.

सुखमास्ते सुखं शेते सुखमायाति याति च।
सुखं वक्ति सुखं भुंक्ते व्यवहारेऽपि शान्तधीः ॥१८-५९॥

sukham aste sukham shete sukham ayati yati cha |
sukham vakti sukham bhunkte vyavahare api shantadhih ||18-59||

He exists in bliss, he sleeps in bliss, he comes and goes in bliss, he talks in bliss, he eats in bliss - such is every action of the peaceful one!

स्वभावाद्यस्य नैवार्तिर्लोकवद् व्यवहारिणः।
महाहृद इवाक्षोभ्यो गतक्लेशः स शोभते ॥१८-६०॥

svabhavad yasya naivartih lokavad vyavaharinah |
mahahruda ivakshobhyo gatakleshah sa shobhate ||18-60||

He who by his very nature does not conduct himself like people of the world shines like a huge lake, in a calm state, with all sorrow gone.

निवृत्तिरपि मूढस्य प्रवृत्ति रुपजायते।
प्रवृत्तिरपि धीरस्य निवृत्तिफलभागिनी ॥१८-६१॥

nivruttirapi mudhasya pravrutti rupajayate |
pravruttirapi dhirasya nivrutti phalabhagini ||18-61||

Even the non-action of a fool takes the form of action. Whereas even the action of a wise man bears the fruit of non-action.

परिग्रहेषु वैराग्यं प्रायो मूढस्य दृश्यते।
देहे विगलिताशस्य क्व रागः क्व विरागता ॥१८-६२॥

parigraheshu vairagyam prayo mudhasya drashyate |
dehe vigalitashasya kva ragah kva viragata ||18-62||

A fool is often seen developing aversion to his possessions. But one whose attachment to the body has melted away, what is attachment to him, and what is detachment?

भावनाभावनासक्ता दृष्टिर्मूढस्य सर्वदा।
भाव्यभावनया सा तु स्वस्थस्याद‍ृष्टिरूपिणी ॥१८-६३॥

bhavan abhavan asakta drashtih mudhasya sarvada |
bhavya abhavanaya sa tu svasthasyadrashti rupini ||18-63||

A fool's vision is always attached to ideas of existence or non-existence. The one of clear vision sees no difference between existence and non-existence.

सर्वारंभेषु निष्कामो यश्चरेद् बालवन् मुनिः।
न लेपस्तस्य शुद्धस्य क्रियमाणोऽपि कर्मणि ॥१८-६४॥

sarvarambheshu nishkamo yaschared balavan munih |
na lepastasya shuddhasya kriyamano api karmani ||18-64||

For the pure sage who remains innocent as a child, and remains without desire in every endeavour, does not get attached even when he performs actions.

स एव धन्य आत्मज्ञः सर्वभावेषु यः समः।
पश्यन् शृण्वन् स्पृशन् जिघ्रन्न् अश्नन्निस्तर्षमानसः ॥१८-६५॥

sa eva dhanya atmagyah sarvabhaveshu yah samah |
pashyan shrunvan sprushan jighrann ashnat nistarsha manasah ||18-65||

The blessed one who knows himself, and is the same in all states remains without desire while seeing, hearing, touching, smelling or eating.

क्व संसारः क्व चाभासः क्व साध्यं क्व च साधनं।
आकाशस्येव धीरस्य निर्विकल्पस्य सर्वदा ॥१८-६६॥

kva sansarah kva chabhasah kva sadhyam kva cha sadhanam |
akashasyeva dhirasya nirvikalpasya sarvada ||18-66||

Where is samsara, and where is fallacy, where is the goal to be achieved, and where are the tools for the wise one who is vast as the sky, and always free of imagination!

स जयत्यर्थसंन्यासी पूर्णस्वरसविग्रहः।
अकृत्रिमोऽनवच्छिन्ने समाधिर्यस्य वर्तते ॥१८-६७॥

sa jayati arthasannyasi purnasvarasavigraha |
akrutrimo anavachhinne samadhiryasya vartate ||18-67||

That sannyasi is victorious who embodies total completeness in himself, who is not artificial, who is not divided, and who does everything in the state of Samadhi.

बहुनात्र किमुक्तेन ज्ञाततत्त्वो महाशयः।
भोगमोक्षनिराकांक्षी सदा सर्वत्र नीरसः ॥१८-६८॥

bahunatra kimuktena gyata tattvo mahashayah |
bhoga moksha nirakankshi sada sarvatra nirasah ||18-68||

What more is there to say of the great man who has realized the truth? He is indifferent to enjoyment or liberation, he is always totally unattached.

महदादि जगद्द्वैतं नाममात्रविजृंभितं।
विहाय शुद्धबोधस्य किं कृत्यमवशिष्यते ॥१८-६९॥

mahad adi jagad dvaitam namamatra vijrumbhitam |
vihaya shuddhabodhasya kim krutyam avashishyate ||18-69||

Having abandoned the mighty heaven as well as this world, and everything that can be extended a name, what can the non-dual one who is pure consciousness be desirous of?

भ्रमभृतमिदं सर्वं किंचिन्नास्तीति निश्चयी।
अलक्ष्यस्फुरणः शुद्धः स्वभावेनैव शाम्यति ॥१८-७०॥

bhram abhrutam idam sarvam kinchit nasti iti nishchayi |
alakshya sfuranah shuddhah svabhavena eva shamyati ||18-70||

The pure one who has naturally attained peace, and who shines without any purpose, has firmly decided that everything is born of illusion, and that nothing actually is.

शुद्धस्फुरणरूपस्य दृश्यभावमपश्यतः।
क्व विधिः क्व वैराग्यं क्व त्यागः क्व शमोऽपि वा ॥१८-७१॥

shuddhasfurana rupasya drashyabhavam apashyatah |
kva vidhih kva vairagyam kva tyagah kva shamo api va ||18-71||

For the pure one shining radiantly who acknowledges no state of being that is visible, what is ritual, what is renunciation, what is sacrifice, and what is cessation?

स्फुरतोऽनन्तरूपेण प्रकृतिं च न पश्यतः।
क्व बन्धः क्व च वा मोक्षः क्व हर्षः क्व विषादिता ॥१८-७२॥

sfurato anantarupena prakrutim cha na pashyatah |
kva bandhah kva cha va mokshah kva harshah kva vishadita ||18-72||

For the one who shines with the radiance of eternity, and who does not acknowledge nature, what is bondage, what is liberation, what is delight, and what is sorrow?

बुद्धिपर्यन्तसंसारे मायामात्रं विवर्तते।
निर्ममो निरहंकारो निष्कामः शोभते बुधः ॥१८-७३॥

buddhiparyanta sansare mayamatram vivartate |
nirmamo nirahankaro nishkamah shobhate budhah ||18-73||

Until consciousness awakens, only Maya plays in this world. But the enlightened one shines free of "I", without ego, without desire.

अक्षयं गतसन्तापमात्मानं पश्यतो मुनेः।
क्व विद्या च क्व वा विश्वं क्व देहोऽहं ममेति वा ॥१८-७४॥

akshayam gatasantapam atmanam pashyato muneh |
kva vidya cha kva va vishvam kva deho aham mameti va ||18-74||

For the sage who knows the self as imperishable and beyond sorrow, where is knowledge, where is the world, where is the sense that "I am the body" or that "The body is mine"?

निरोधादीनि कर्माणि जहाति जडधीर्यदि।
मनोरथान् प्रलापांश्च कर्तुमाप्नोत्यतत्क्षणात् ॥१८-७५॥

nirodhadini karmani jahati jadadhiryadi |
manorathan pralapanshcha kartum apnoti atatkshanat ||18-75||

As soon as the fool stops actions like cessation of thought, at that very moment, he goes back to chasing the mind's desires and chatter.

मन्दः श्रुत्वापि तद्वस्तु न जहाति विमूढताम्।
निर्विकल्पो बहिर्यत्नादन्तर्विषयलालसः ॥१८-७६॥

mandah shrutvapi tadvastu na jahati vimudhatam |
nirvikalpo bahiryatnad antarvishayalalasah ||18-76||

The fool is not rid of foolishness even on hearing the truth. He may seem desireless from outside, but from within, he lusts after sense-objects.

ज्ञानाद् गलितकर्मा यो लोकदृष्ट्यापि कर्मकृत्।
नाप्नोत्यवसरं कर्म वक्तुमेव न किंचन ॥१८-७७॥

gyanad galitakarma yo lokadrashtyapi karmakrut |
napnoti avasaram karmam vaktumeva na kinchana ||18-77||

The wise one whose karma has melted away may still seem active in the eyes of the world, but he comes across no occasion for doing or speaking anything.

क्व तमः क्व प्रकाशो वा हानं क्व च न किंचन।
निर्विकारस्य धीरस्य निरातंकस्य सर्वदा ॥१८-७८॥

kva tamah kva prakasho va hanam kva cha na kinchana |
nirvikarasya dhirasya niratankasya sarvada ||18-78||

What is darkness, what is light, what is injury to the wise one who is forever unchanging and without pain?

क्व धैर्यं क्व विवेकित्वं क्व निरातंकतापि वा।
अनिर्वाच्यस्वभावस्य निःस्वभावस्य योगिनः ॥१८-७९॥

kva dhairyam kva vivekitvam kva niratankatapi va |
anirvachya svabhavasya nihsvabhavasya yoginah ||18-79||

What is courage, what is discrimination, what is painlessness to the yogi who is blameless by nature and who is free of personality?

न स्वर्गो नैव नरको जीवन्मुक्तिर्न चैव हि।
बहुनात्र किमुक्तेन योगदृष्ट्या न किंचन ॥१८-८०॥

na svargo naiva narako jivanmuktirna chaiva hi |
bahunatra kimuktena yogadrashtya na kinchana ||18-80||

There is neither heaven nor hell, nor even liberation from life. What more is there to say – in yogic vision, there is nothing!

नैव प्रार्थयते लाभं नालाभेनानुशोचति।
धीरस्य शीतलं चित्तममृतेनैव पूरितम् ॥१८-८१॥

naiva prarthayate labham nalabhena anushochati |
dhirasya shitalam chittam amrutena eva puritam ||18-81||

The wise, calm one who is replete with the nectar of consciousness neither prays for gain, nor laments loss.

न शान्तं स्तौति निष्कामो न दुष्टमपि निन्दति।
समदुःखसुखस्तृप्तः किंचित् कृत्यं न पश्यति ॥१८-८२॥

na shantam stauti nishkamo na dushtam api nindati |
samadukha sukhastruptah kinchit krutyam na pashyati ||18-82||

The desireless one neither praises the good nor condemns the wicked. Staying equally contented in joy or sorrow, he sees nothing that needs action.

धीरो न द्वेष्टि संसारमात्मानं न दिदृक्षति।
हर्षामर्षविनिर्मुक्तो न मृतो न च जीवति ॥१८-८३॥

dhiro na dveshti sansaram atmanam na didrakshati |
harshamarsha vinirmukto na mruto na cha jivati ||18-83||

The wise one is not repulsed by samsara, nor desires to know the Self. He is free of delight as well as indignation, he is neither dead nor alive.

निःस्नेहः पुत्रदारादौ निष्कामो विषयेषु च।
निश्चिन्तः स्वशरीरेऽपि निराशः शोभते बुधः ॥१८-८४॥

nihsnehah putrid aradau nishkamo vishayeshu cha |
nishchintah svasharire api nirashah shobhate budhah ||18-84||

The wise one is unattached to children or wife, and has no desire for sense objects. He shines in a state without hope, and unconcerned with his own body.

तुष्टिः सर्वत्र धीरस्य यथापतितवर्तिनः।
स्वच्छन्दं चरतो देशान् यत्रस्तमितशायिनः ॥१८-८५॥

tushtih sarvatra dhirasya yathapatitavartinah |
svachhandam charato deshan yatrastam itashayinah ||18-85||

There is peace everywhere for the wise one who engages in whatever falls into his plate, who goes wherever he wants of his free will, who sleeps wherever the sun sets.

पततूदेतु वा देहो नास्य चिन्ता महात्मनः ।
स्वभावभूमिविश्रान्तिविस्मृताशेषसंसृतेः ॥१८- ८६॥

etat udetu va deho nasya chinta mahatmanah |
svabhava bhumivishranti vismrutashesha sansruteh ||18-86||

The great one is not worried whether his body has fallen or risen. He rests on the ground of his true nature, and forgets this entire samsara!

अकिंचनः कामचारो निर्द्वन्द्वश्छिन्नसंशयः ।
असक्तः सर्वभावेषु केवलो रमते बुधः ॥१८- ८७॥

akinchanah kamacharo nirdvandvash chinna sanshayah |
asaktah sarvabhaveshu kevalo ramate budhah ||18-87||

Having no possessions, free, without duality, he who has slashed all doubts, who is detached from every emotion plays alone.

निर्ममः शोभते धीरः समलोष्टाश्मकांचनः ।
सुभिन्नहृदयग्रन्थिर्विनिर्धूतरजस्तमः ॥१८- ८८॥

nirmamah shobhate dhirah samaloshtashma kanchanah |
subhinna hridayagranthih vinirdhuta rajastamah ||18-88||

The wise one shines without ego. To him, earth, a stone or gold are the same. The various knots of his heart have been slashed to pieces, and he is free from greed and blindness.

सर्वत्रानवधानस्य न किंचिद् वासना हृदि।
मुक्तात्मनो वितृप्तस्य तुलना केन जायते ॥१८-८९॥

sarvatran avadhanasya na kinchid vasana hridi |
muktatmano vitruptasya tulana kena jayate ||18-89||

Who can be compared to the completely contented, liberated soul who is non-attentive to everything, and who has no lust in his heart?

जानन्नपि न जानाति पश्यन्नपि न पश्यति।
ब्रुवन्न् अपि न च ब्रूते कोऽन्यो निर्वासनादृते ॥१८-९०॥

janannapi na janati pashyannapi na pashyati |
bruvann api na cha brute ka anyo nirvasan adrate ||18-90||

Who else but the upright man without desire does not know in spite of knowing, does not see in spite of seeing, does not speak in spite of speaking?

भिक्षुर्वा भूपतिर्वापि यो निष्कामः स शोभते।
भावेषु गलिता यस्य शोभनाशोभना मतिः ॥१८-९१॥

bhikshurva bhupatirvapi yo nishkamah sa shobhate |
bhaveshu galita yasya shobhana ashobhana matih ||18-91||

The one in whom 'agreeable' and 'disagreeable' - all such states of being have melted away, shines free of desire, whether he is a beggar or a king.

क्व स्वाच्छन्द्यं क्व संकोचः क्व वा तत्त्वविनिश्चयः।
निर्व्याजार्जवभूतस्य चरितार्थस्य योगिनः ॥१८-९२॥

kva svachhandyam kva sankochah kva va tattva vinishchayah |
nirvyaj arjava bhutasya charitarthasya yoginah ||18-92||

What is self-will, what is doubt, what is decidedly the truth for the one who has the character of a yogi, and who is the emobidement of sincerity and honesty!

आत्मविश्रान्तितृप्तेन निराशेन गतार्तिना।
अन्तर्यदनुभूयेत तत् कथं कस्य कथ्यते ॥१८-९३॥

atmavishranti truptena nirashena gatartina |
antaryadanubhuyeta tat katham kasya kathyate ||18-93||

What is there to be said about the internal state of being of the one who is content and rests only in the Self, who is without hope and free of anguish!

सुप्तोऽपि न सुषुप्तौ च स्वप्नेऽपि शयितो न च।
जागरेऽपि न जागर्ति धीरस्तृप्तः पदे पदे ॥१८-९४॥

supto api na sushuptau cha svapne api shayito na cha |
jagare api na jagarti dhirastruptah pade pade ||18-94||

The wise one is content in all states. He does not sleep even when fast asleep, he does not dream even when asleep, he is not awake even in waking!

ज्ञः सचिन्तोऽपि निश्चिन्तः सेन्द्रियोऽपि निरिन्द्रियः।
सुबुद्धिरपि निर्बुद्धिः साहंकारोऽनहङ्कृतिः ॥१८-९५॥

gyah sachinta api nishchintah sa indriyo api nir indriyah |
subuddhirapi nirbuddhih sahankara anahankrutih ||18-95||

The knowing one is without thought even when thinking, without senses even when with senses, intelligent even when appearing foolish, without ego even when appearing egoistic.

न सुखी न च वा दुःखी न विरक्तो न संगवान्।
न मुमुक्षुर्न वा मुक्ता न किंचिन्न च किंचन ॥१८-९६॥

na sukhi na cha va dukhi na virakto na sangavan |
na mumukshurna va mukta na kinchit na cha kinchana ||18-96||

Neither happy nor sad, neither deprived nor in plenty, neither seeking liberation nor free, neither any of these nor anything at all!

विक्षेपेऽपि न विक्षिप्तः समाधौ न समाधिमान्।
जाड्येऽपि न जडो धन्यः पाण्डित्येऽपि न पण्डितः ॥१८-९७॥

vikshepe api na vikshiptah samadhau na samadhiman |
jadye api na jado dhanyah panditye api na panditah ||18-97||

In spite of disturbances he is not agitated, in spite of being in a transcendental state he is not meditative, in spite of being born he is not stupid, in spite of being wise he is not a scholar.

मुक्तो यथास्थितिस्वस्थः कृतकर्तव्यनिर्वृतः ।
समः सर्वत्र वैतृष्ण्यान्न स्मरत्यकृतं कृतम् ॥१८-९८॥

mukto yathasthiti svasthah kruta kartavya nirvrutah |
samah sarvatra vaitrushni anna smarati akrutam krutam ||18-98||

He is free and established in whatever condition he is, whether he is doing his duty or free from it. He is the same everywhere, and free from desire, and has no remembrance of what he did or did not do.

न प्रीयते वन्द्यमानो निन्द्यमानो न कुप्यति ।
नैवोद्विजति मरणे जीवने नाभिनन्दति ॥१८-९९॥

na priyate vandyamano nindyamano na kupyati |
naivodvijati marane jivane nabhinandati ||18-99||

He is not pleased when he is worshipped, and is not enraged when he is demeaned. Neither does he grieve in death, nor is he congratulatory in life.

न धावति जनाकीर्णं नारण्यं उपशान्तधीः ।
यथातथा यत्रतत्र सम एवावतिष्ठते ॥१८-१००॥

na dhavati janakirna naranyam upashantadhih |
yathatatha yatratatra sama evavatishthate ||18-100||

The wise, tranquil one does not flee to a place crowded with people, or to a forest. He stands the same exactly the way he is and where he is.

Chapter 19

जनक उवाच-
तत्त्वविज्ञानसन्दंशमादाय हृदयोदरात्।
नानाविधपरामर्शशल्योद्धारः कृतो मया ॥१९-१॥

janaka uvacha
tattva vigyana sandamsham adaya hrudayodarat |
nanavidha paramarsha shalyoddharah kruto maya ||19-1||

Janaka said –
With the pincers of the highest truth, I have extracted violent thorns of various kinds out of my heart.

क्व धर्मः क्व च वा कामः क्व चार्थः क्व विवेकिता।
क्व द्वैतं क्व च वाऽद्वैतं स्वमहिम्नि स्थितस्य मे ॥१९-२॥

kva dharmah kva cha va kamah kva charthah kva vivekita |
kva dvaitam kva cha va advaitam svamahimni sthitasya me ||19-2||

What is righteousness, what is desire, what is wealth, what is discrimination, what is duality or non-duality to me who stands steady in myself?

क्व भूतं क्व भविष्यद् वा वर्तमानमपि क्व वा।
क्व देशः क्व च वा नित्यं स्वमहिम्नि स्थितस्य मे ॥१९-३॥

kva bhutam kva bhavishyad va vartamanam api kva va |
kva deshah kva cha va nityam svamahimni sthitasya me ||19-3||

What is the past, what is the future, what is the present, what is space or time to me, who stands steady in myself?

क्व चात्मा क्व च वानात्मा क्व शुभं क्वाशुभं तथा।
क्व चिन्ता क्व च वाचिन्ता स्वमहिम्नि स्थितस्य मे ॥१९-४॥

kva cha atma kva cha vanatma kva shubham kva shubham tatha |
kva chinta kva cha vachinta svamahimni sthitasya me ||19-4||

What is the soul, what is not the soul, what is good or bad, what is thought or lack of thought to me who stands steady in myself?

क्व स्वप्नः क्व सुषुप्तिर्वा क्व च जागरणं तथा।
क्व तुरियं भयं वापि स्वमहिम्नि स्थितस्य मे ॥१९-५॥

kva svapnah kva sushuptirva kva cha jagaranam tatha |
kva turiyam bhayam vapi svam ahimni sthitasya me ||19-5||

What is dreaming, what is sleep, what is waking, what is the 'state of witnessing' or fear to me, who stands steady in myself?

क्व दूरं क्व समीपं वा बाह्यं क्वाभ्यन्तरं क्व वा।
क्व स्थूलं क्व च वा सूक्ष्मं स्वमहिम्नि स्थितस्य मे ॥१९-६॥

kva duram kva samipam va bahyam kva abhyantaram kva va |
kva sthulam kva cha va sukshmam svamahimni sthitasya me ||19-6||

What is distance, what is closeness, what is without or within, what is manifest, what is subtle to me, who stands steady in myself?

क्व मृत्युर्जीवितं वा क्व लोकाः क्वास्य क्व लौकिकं।
क्व लयः क्व समाधिर्वा स्वमहिम्नि स्थितस्य मे ॥१९-७॥

kva mrutyurjivitam va kva lokah kvasya kva laukikam |
kva layah kva samadhirva svamahimni sthitasya me ||19-7||

What is death or life, what is this world or worldliness, what is spiritual indifference or a state of Samadhi to me, who stands steady in myself?

अलं त्रिवर्गकथया योगस्य कथयाप्यलं।
अलं विज्ञानकथया विश्रान्तस्य ममात्मनि ॥१९-८॥

alam trivargakathaya yogasya kathayapyalam |
alam vigyana kathaya vishrantasya mamatmani ||19-8||

Enough talking about the three classifications (of goals), enough talking about yoga, enough talking about wisdom! I rest in myself!

Chapter 20

जनक उवाच -
क्व भूतानि क्व देहो वा क्वेन्द्रियाणि क्व वा मनः ।
क्व शून्यं क्व च नैराश्यं मत्स्वरूपे निरंजने ॥२०-१॥

janaka uvacha
kva bhutani kva deho va kva indriyani kva va manah |
kva shunyam kva cha nairashyam matsvarupe niranjane ||20-1||

Janaka said –
What are people, what is body, what are senses, what is the mind, what is nothingness, and what is desirelessness to my stainless state?

क्व शास्त्रं क्वात्मविज्ञानं क्व वा निर्विषयं मनः ।
क्व तृप्तिः क्व वितृष्णत्वं गतद्वन्द्वस्य मे सदा ॥२०- २॥

kva shastram kva atmavigyanam kva va nirvishayam manah |
kva truptih kva vitrushnatvam gata dvandvasya me sada ||20-2||

What are scriptures, what is self-knowledge, what is satisfaction or a mind without senses, what is the state of desirelessness to me in whom duality has forever disappeared?

क्व विद्या क्व च वाविद्या क्वाहं क्वेदं मम क्व वा ।
क्व बन्ध क्व च वा मोक्षः स्वरूपस्य क्व रूपिता ॥२०- ३॥

kva vidya kva cha vavidya kvaham kvedam mama kva va |
kva bandha kva va mokshah svarupasya kva rupita ||20-3||

What is knowledge, what is ignorance, what is 'me', and what is this 'mine', what is bondage and what is liberation, what is the appearance of the Self?

क्व प्रारब्धानि कर्माणि जीवन्मुक्तिरपि क्व वा।
क्व तद् विदेहकैवल्यं निर्विशेषस्य सर्वदा ॥२०-४॥

kva prarabdhani karmani jivanmuktirapi kva va |
kva tad videha kaivalyam nirvisheshasya sarvada ||20-4||

What is endeavour, what is liberation from life, what is perfect beatitude by detachment from the body, there is never any distinction amongst any state!

क्व कर्ता क्व च वा भोक्ता निष्क्रियं स्फुरणं क्व वा।
क्वापरोक्षं फलं वा क्व निःस्वभावस्य मे सदा ॥२०-५॥

kva karta kva cha va bhokta nishkriyam sfuranam kva va |
kvaparoksham phalam va kva nihsvabhavasya me sada ||20-5||

What is the doer, what is the experiencer, what is inactivity or springing up, what is beyond vision, what is reward, I am forever the one without personality!

क्व लोकं क्व मुमुक्षुर्वा क्व योगी ज्ञानवान् क्व वा।
क्व बद्धः क्व च वा मुक्तः स्वस्वरूपेऽहमद्वये ॥२०-६॥

kva lokam kva mumukshurva kva yogi gyanavan kva va |
kva baddhah kva cha va muktah svasvarupe ahamadvaye ||20-6||

What is this world, what is the desire for liberation, what is a yogi, what is a wise man, what is bondage, what is liberation, I am non-dual by my very nature!

क्व सृष्टिः क्व च संहारः क्व साध्यं क्व च साधनं।
क्व साधकः क्व सिद्धिर्वा स्वस्वरूपेऽहमद्वये ॥२०-७॥

kva srushtih kva cha sanharah kva sadhyam kva cha sadhanam |
kva sadhakah kva siddhirva svasvarupe ahamadvaye ||20-7||

What is creation, what is destruction, what is to be achieved and what is the tool, what is the achiever, and what is achievement, I am non-dual by my very nature!

क्व प्रमाता प्रमाणं वा क्व प्रमेयं क्व च प्रमा।
क्व किंचित् क्व न किंचिद् वा सर्वदा विमलस्य मे ॥२०-८॥

kva pramata pramanam va kva premayam kva cha prama |
kva kinchit kva na kinchid va sarvada vimalasya me ||20-8||

What is the prover or proof, what is to be measured and what is the measure, what is something or nothing – I am always pure!

क्व विक्षेपः क्व चैकाग्र्यं क्व निर्बोधः क्व मूढता।
क्व हर्षः क्व विषादो वा सर्वदा निष्क्रियस्य मे ॥२०-९॥

kva vikshepah kva cha ekagnyam kva nirbodhah kva mudhata |
kva harshah kva vishado va sarvada nishkriyasya me ||20-9||

What is distraction, what is concentration, what is stupidity or ignorance, what is delight or sorrow, I am forever actionless.

क्व चैष व्यवहारो वा क्व च सा परमार्थता।
क्व सुखं क्व च वा दुखं निर्विमर्शस्य मे सदा ॥२०-१०॥

kva chaisha vyavaharo va kva cha sa paramarthata |
kva sukham kva cha va dukham nirvimarshasya me sada ||20-10||

What is conduct, what is the highest truth, what is joy and what is sorrow, I am forever beyond analysis.

क्व माया क्व च संसारः क्व प्रीतिर्विरतिः क्व वा।
क्व जीवः क्व च तद्ब्रह्म सर्वदा विमलस्य मे ॥२०-११॥

kva maya kva cha sansarah kva pritirviratih kva va |
kva jivah kva cha tadbrahma sarvada vimalasya me ||20-11||

What is maya, what is samsara, what is liking or disliking, what is a living being, what is the Absolute, I am forever stainless.

क्व प्रवृत्तिर्निर्वृत्तिर्वा क्व मुक्तिः क्व च बन्धनं।
कूटस्थनिर्विभागस्य स्वस्थस्य मम सर्वदा ॥२०-१२॥

kva pravruttih nirvruttirva kva muktih kva cha bandhanam |
kutastha nirvibhagasya svasthasya mama sarvada ||20-12||

What is action or inaction, what is liberation and what is bondage, I am forever unchanging, indivisible, complete!

क्वोपदेशः क्व वा शास्त्रं क्व शिष्यः क्व च वा गुरुः।
क्व चास्ति पुरुषार्थो वा निरुपाधेः शिवस्य मे ॥२०-१३॥

kva upadeshah kva va shastram kva shishyah kva va guruh |
kva cha asti purushartho va nirupadheh shivasya me ||20-13||

What is teaching, what is scripture, what is student or teacher, what is hard work, I am the formless Shiva.

क्व चास्ति क्व च वा नास्ति क्वास्ति चैकं क्व च द्वयं।
बहुनात्र किमुक्तेन किंचिन्नोतिष्ठते मम ॥२०-१४॥

kva cha asti kva cha va nasti kvasti cha ekam kva cha dvayam |
bahunatra kim uktena kinchit na uttishthate mama ||20-14||

What is existence or non-existence, what is non-duality or duality, what more is there to say? Nothing else arises from me!

The End.

ॐ

Printed in Great Britain
by Amazon